THE CHRYSOSTOM BIBLE
A Commentary Series for Preaching and Teaching
Ephesians & 2 Thessalonians: A Commentary

THE CHRYSOSTOM BIBLE
A Commentary Series for Preaching and Teaching

Ephesians & 2 Thessalonians: A Commentary

Paul Nadim Tarazi

OCABS PRESS
ST PAUL, MINNESOTA 55124
2019

To Xavier, Emile, and Marcel

THE CHRYSOSTOM BIBLE
EPHESIANS & 2 THESSALONIANS: A COMMENTARY

Copyright © 2019 by
Paul Nadim Tarazi

ISBN 1-60191-047-9

PRINTED IN THE UNITED STATES OF AMERICA

Other Books by the Author

I Thessalonians: A Commentary
Galatians: A Commentary

The Old Testament: An Introduction
Volume 1: Historical Traditions, revised edition
Volume 2: Prophetic Traditions
Volume 3: Psalms and Wisdom

The New Testament: An Introduction
Volume 1: Paul and Mark
Volume 2: Luke and Acts
Volume 3: Johannine Writings
Volume 4: Matthew and the Canon

The Chrysostom Bible

Genesis: A Commentary
Philippians: A Commentary
Romans: A Commentary
Colossians & Philemon: A Commentary
1 Corinthians: A Commentary
Ezekiel: A Commentary
Joshua: A Commentary
2 Corinthians: A Commentary
Isaiah: A Commentary
Jeremiah: A Commentary
Hebrews: A Commentary
The Pastorals: A Commentary

Land and Covenant

The Rise of Scripture

The Chrysostom Bible
Ephesians & 2 Thessalonians: A Commentary

ISBN 1-60191-047-9

Published by OCABS Press, St. Paul, Minnesota.
Printed in the United States of America.

Books are available through OCABS Press at special discounts for
bulk purchases in the United States by academic institutions,
churches, and other organizations. For more information please
email OCABS Press at press@ocabs.org.

Abbreviations

Books by the Author

1 Thess   *I Thessalonians: A Commentary*, Crestwood, NY: St. Vladimir's Seminary Press, 1982

Gal   *Galatians: A Commentary*, Crestwood, NY: St. Vladimir's Seminary Press, 1994

OTI₁   *The Old Testament: An Introduction, Volume 1: Historical Traditions*, revised edition, Crestwood, NY: St. Vladimir's Seminary Press, 2003

OTI₂   *The Old Testament: An Introduction, Volume 2: Prophetic Traditions*, Crestwood, NY: St. Vladimir's Seminary Press, 1994

OTI₃   *The Old Testament: An Introduction, Volume 3: Psalms and Wisdom*, Crestwood, NY: St. Vladimir's Seminary Press, 1996

NTI₁   *The New Testament: An Introduction, Volume 1: Paul and Mark*, Crestwood, NY: St. Vladimir's Seminary Press, 1999

NTI₂   *The New Testament: An Introduction, Volume 2: Luke and Acts*, Crestwood, NY: St. Vladimir's Seminary Press, 2001

NTI₃   *The New Testament: An Introduction, Volume 3: Johannine Writings*, Crestwood, NY: St. Vladimir's Seminary Press, 2004

NTI₄   *The New Testament: An Introduction, Volume 4: Matthew and the Canon*, St. Paul, MN: OCABS Press, 2009

C-Gen   *Genesis: A Commentary*. The Chrysostom Bible. St. Paul, MN: OCABS Press, 2009

C-Phil   *Philippians: A Commentary*. The Chrysostom Bible. St. Paul, MN: OCABS Press, 2009

C-Rom   *Romans: A Commentary*. The Chrysostom Bible. St. Paul, MN: OCABS Press, 2010

C-Col   *Colossians & Philemon: A Commentary*. The Chrysostom Bible. St. Paul, MN: OCABS Press, 2010

C-1Cor   *1 Corinthians: A Commentary*. The Chrysostom Bible. St. Paul, MN: OCABS Press, 2011

C-Ezek   *Ezekiel: A Commentary*. The Chrysostom Bible. St. Paul, MN: OCABS Press, 2012

C-Josh   *Joshua: A Commentary*. The Chrysostom Bible. St. Paul, MN: OCABS Press, 2013

C-2Cor   *2 Corinthians: A Commentary*. The Chrysostom Bible. St. Paul, MN: OCABS Press, 2013

C-Is   *Isaiah: A Commentary*. The Chrysostom Bible. St. Paul, MN: OCABS Press, 2013

C-Jer   *Jeremiah: A Commentary.* The Chrysostom Bible. St. Paul, MN: OCABS Press, 2013

C-Heb   *Hebrews: A Commentary.* The Chrysostom Bible. St. Paul, MN: OCABS Press, 2014

C-Pas   *The Pastorals: A Commentary.* The Chrysostom Bible. St. Paul, MN: OCABS Press, 2016

LAC   *Land and Covenant,* St. Paul, MN: OCABS Press, 2009

ROS   *The Rise of Scripture,* St. Paul, MN: OCABS Press, 2017

Abbreviations

Books of the Old Testament*

Gen	Genesis	Job	Job	Hab	Habakkuk
Ex	Exodus	Ps	Psalms	Zeph	Zephaniah
Lev	Leviticus	Prov	Proverbs	Hag	Haggai
Num	Numbers	Eccl	Ecclesiastes	Zech	Zechariah
Deut	Deuteronomy	Song	Song of Solomon	Mal	Malachi
Josh	Joshua	Is	Isaiah	Tob	Tobit
Judg	Judges	Jer	Jeremiah	Jdt	Judith
Ruth	Ruth	Lam	Lamentations	Wis	Wisdom
1 Sam	1 Samuel	Ezek	Ezekiel	Sir	Sirach (Ecclesiasticus
2 Sam	2 Samuel	Dan	Daniel	Bar	)
1 Kg	1 Kings	Hos	Hosea	1 Esd	Baruch
2 Kg	2 Kings	Joel	Joel	2 Esd	1 Esdras
1 Chr	1 Chronicles	Am	Amos	1 Macc	2 Esdras
2 Chr	2 Chronicles	Ob	Obadiah	2 Macc	1 Maccabees
Ezra	Ezra	Jon	Jonah	3 Macc	2 Maccabees
Neh	Nehemiah	Mic	Micah	4 Macc	3 Maccabees
Esth	Esther	Nah	Nahum		4 Maccabees

Books of the New Testament

Mt	Matthew	Eph	Ephesians	Heb	Hebrews
Mk	Mark	Phil	Philippians	Jas	James
Lk	Luke	Col	Colossians	1 Pet	1 Peter
Jn	John	1 Thess	1 Thessalonians	2 Pet	2 Peter
Acts	Acts	2 Thess	2 Thessalonians	1 Jn	1 John
Rom	Romans	1 Tim	1 Timothy	2 Jn	2 John
1 Cor	1 Corinthians	2 Tim	2 Timothy	3 Jn	3 John
2 Cor	2 Corinthians	Titus	Titus	Jude	Jude
Gal	Galatians	Philem	Philemon	Rev	Revelation

Following the larger canon known as the Septuagint.

Contents

Foreword

With this book Fr. Paul Nadim Tarazi concludes a cycle of commentaries on the entire *corpus paulinum*, a life-long project that began in 1982 with the inaugural publication of his commentary on 1 Thessalonians. A detailed exegetical commentary of Galatians followed in 1994, which is one of Tarazi's most extensive works and is a volume rich in contributions to Pauline research. From then on, his commentaries on Paul's epistles would continue in the prestigious Chrysostom Bible series. First in this series was the commentary on Philippians in 2009, and today the cycle closes with this double volume on Ephesians and 2 Thessalonians.

In this commentary, Father Tarazi masterfully combines the pastoral message with an in-depth analysis of the original Greek text. The outcome is an enjoyable and accessible book for those people who have a particular interest in discovering the treasures of two New Testament letters that contributed to the formation of our Christian identity. The biblical text is present at the beginning of each chapter in both Greek and English, a feature that allows the readers to comfortably handle both texts in a single book. The presence of the Greek text should not discourage a non-specialized reader since everything is clearly explained in English. When the Greek terms are interpreted, the author presents them in italics so that they are perfectly identifiable and immediately translated, e.g., "managed plan" for *oikonomia* or "commonwealth" for *politevma*.

Tarazi possesses an extensive knowledge of Scripture in both Testaments and guides his readers to consult Prophetic Books, the Gospels, the Psalms and the Law to see the connectivity of the entire bible. He continues this approach in this commentary to show us how the writer of Ephesians and 2 Thessalonians read and understood earlier scriptural books, and also to show how other New Testament authors presented and explained the announcement of the Christian faith from the Pauline tradition.

Father Tarazi is very aware of what is written and discussed in biblical scholarship worldwide and his work addresses some of these topics without distracting his readers with the academic formalities of bibliographical citations and references. He does this to ease the reading and comprehension of the message he is conferring. Thus, for example, in the introduction to Ephesians, some paragraphs are dedicated to showing the literary relationship between this epistle and Colossians. He explains this specific question not only from the historical and geographical point of view, considering that both cities belonged to the same Roman province, but also from the interlinkage of topics and literary style. He considers, for instance, the mention of Nympha, whose name means bride, and "the church in her house" in Col 4:15 as a literary allusion to the church of Ephesus and its epistle where the community is presented as Christ's "bride" (Eph 5:22-33). Tarazi gives a central function to the community of Ephesus, which he calls "the Pauline headquarters," and considers the epistle to the Ephesians as "the complete and comprehensive missive of the entire Pauline teaching."

The book's dynamics consist of following the thread of the Pauline writing chapter after chapter. It is the text that proposes the topics to be discussed and explained. Tarazi interlinks the commentary with parallel Pauline texts and explains the message for his readers. He also comments on those Greek terms and phrases that are not accurately reflected in the English translations of the Bible, but are essential to understanding the original message within its cultural context.

Another aspect of importance is the canonical approach opted by Tarazi to explain the epistles. In other words, he interprets while indicating step by step the function that each missive fulfills in its assigned place within the New Testament canon. He shows how some key terms are present in one book and then are found in another book, and explains how these terms develop a particular theological theme. For instance, he proposes an interaction between 1 and 2 Thessalonians and claims that the term Gospel in the second epistle deals with the topic of the coming of the Lord that was already dealt with in 1 Thessalonians 4:13-5:11 and was not properly heard. Thus, the second epistle goes back to this subject three times, following the scriptural model of didactic repetition and as a warning to "the forthcoming judgment of all" already mentioned in the opening of the Pauline collection in Romans 2:16.

In the formal milieu of contemporary biblical scholarship, this book may seem unconventional because it neither conforms to the typical norms of a commentary, nor respects the limits and formalities of an introduction. Those who know the work of Father Tarazi and have attended his lectures and sermons, listened to his podcasts at ephesusschool.org, and followed his pastoral courses in so many Orthodox parishes in America and abroad, will hear in this book the living word that enlightens heart and mind and gives strength with its message. This book is an unrivaled reference tool for pastors preparing their sermons and for Bible study groups who will find it a useful and precise commentary and will also be able to find in it references to parallel and explanatory texts in other Pauline and non-Pauline books of the Bible.

The text that we have in our hands presents a convincing and well-argued explanation of two Pauline missives. To Orthodox in particular and to every Christian, in general, it is a call to keep delving into the reading of Holy Scripture and rediscovering its place in the life of the church.

In this sense the book fulfills the key mission of the "Chrysostom Bible" series which is to continue the legacy of this great Antiochian saint and exegete in his pastoral work of teaching the believers day by day and of remembering the enthusiasm they experienced in the first days when they embraced the Christian faith, and keeping the torch alive in their hearts. With this collection of books on the Pauline writings, Father Paul Tarazi gives us an update of this typically Antiochian legacy of reading continuously and repetitively the Scriptures, which are, as Chrysostom said, "an inexhaustible source of life" (PG 48: 1007).

Daniel Ayuch

Preface

The present Bible Commentary Series is not so much in honor of John Chrysostom as it is to continue and promote his legacy as an interpreter of the biblical texts for preaching and teaching God's congregation, in order to prod its members to proceed on the way they started when they accepted God's calling. Chrysostom's virtual uniqueness is that he did not subscribe to any hermeneutic or methodology, since this would amount to introducing an extra-textual authority over the biblical texts. For him, scripture is its own interpreter. Listening to the texts time and again allowed him to realize that "call" and "read (aloud)" are not interconnected realities; rather, they are one reality since they both are renditions of the same Hebrew verb *qara*'. Given that words read aloud are words of instruction for one "to do them," the only valid reaction would be to hear, listen, obey, and abide by these words. All these connotations are subsumed in the same Hebrew verb *šama*'. On the other hand, these scriptural "words of life" are presented as readily understandable utterances of a father to his children (Isaiah 1:2-3). The recipients are never asked to engage in an intellectual debate with their divine instructor, or even among themselves, to fathom what he is saying. The Apostle to the Gentiles followed in the footsteps of the Prophets to Israel by handing down to them the Gospel, that is, the Law of God's Spirit through his Christ (Romans 8:2; Galatians 6:2) as fatherly instruction (1 Corinthians 4:15). He in turn wrote readily understandable letters to be read aloud. It is in these same footsteps that Chrysostom followed, having learned from both the Prophets and Paul that the same "words of life" carry also the sentence of death at the hand of the scriptural God, Judge of all (Deuteronomy 28; Joshua 8:32-35; Psalm 82; Matthew 3:4-12; Romans 2:12-16; 1 Corinthians 10:1-11; Revelation 20:11-15).

While theological debates and hermeneutical theories come and go after having fed their proponents and their fans with passing human glory, the Golden Mouth's expository homilies, through the centuries, fed and still feed myriads of believers in so many traditions and countries. Virtually banned from dogmatic treatises, he survives in the hearts of "those who have ears to hear." His success is due to his commitment to exegesis rather than to futile hermeneutics. The latter behaves as someone who dictates on a living organism what it is supposed to be, whereas exegesis submits to that organism and endeavors to decipher it through trial and error. There is as much a far cry between the text and the theories about it as there is between a living organism and the theories about it. The biblical texts are the reality of God imparted through their being read aloud in the midst of the congregation, disregarding the value of the sermon that follows. The sermon, much less a theological treatise, is at best an invitation to hear and obey the text. Assessing the shape of an invitation card has no value whatsoever when it comes to the dinner itself; the guests are fed by the dinner, not by the invitation or its phrasing (Luke 14:16-24; Matthew 22:1-14).

This commentary series does not intend to promote Chrysostom's ideas as a public relation manager would do, but rather to follow in the footsteps of his approach as true children and heirs are expected to do. He used all the contemporary tools at his disposal to communicate God's written instruction to his hearers, as a doctor would with his patients, without spending unnecessary energy on peripheral debates requiring the use of professional jargon incomprehensible to the commoner. The writers of this series will try to do the same: muster to the best of their ability all necessary contemporary knowledge to communicate to the general readers the biblical message without burdening them with data unnecessary for that purpose. Whenever it will be deemed necessary or even helpful to do so, and in order to curtail burdensome and lengthy technical asides within the commentaries, specialized monographs related either to specific topics or to the scriptural background—literary, socio-political, or archeological—will be issued as companions to the series.

Paul Nadim Tarazi
Editor

Ephesians

Introduction

The Pauline corpus is conceived as a literarily structured whole. The letters are clustered into units through the repetition of a "signature" that appears as a refrain at the end of each literary unit. At the end of the second and the fourth major epistles we read:

I, Paul, write this greeting with my own hand. (1 Cor 16:21)

See with what large letters I am writing to you with my own hand. (Gal 6:11)

At the end of the three captivity epistles to churches we read:

I, Paul, write this greeting with my own hand. (Col 4:18)

At the end of the epistles to the Thessalonians we read:

I, Paul, write this greeting with my own hand. *This is the mark in every letter of mine; it is the way I write.* (2 Thess 3:17)

At the end of the four letters to individuals we read:

I, Paul, write this with my own hand. (Philem 1:19)

It is evident that the letters to churches form a literary unit separate from the letters to individuals. "The mark in every letter of mine" at the end of 2 Thessalonians suggests the completeness of the letters in this literary unit. These letters to churches form a set of nine writings, the center of which is the epistle to the Ephesians. The position of centrality of that epistle makes sense since it encompasses the totality of Paul's message. Its most important elements are taken from Romans, 1 and 2 Corinthians, and Galatians.

Unique to Ephesians is that early manuscripts reflect two readings: one that has the phrase "in Ephesus" after "to the saints who are" and another reading that omits the phrase:

Paul, an apostle of Jesus Christ by the will of God, to the saints which are at Ephesus, and to the faithful in Christ Jesus (Eph 1:1 KJV)

Paul, an apostle of Christ Jesus by the will of God, To the saints who are also faithful in Christ Jesus (Eph 1:1 RSV)

It is difficult to decide whether the phrase was "added" to an original or it was "omitted" from an original, since both readings are attested to in a number of reliable manuscripts. However, whether the writing was originally conceived as a "universal" letter or as one addressed to Ephesus, which is—scripturally speaking—the Pauline headquarters, the result is the same: Ephesians is both the complete and comprehensive missive of the entire Pauline teaching. Listening to it presents the hearer with the entire message of scripture.

The universality of the letter actually corresponds to scriptural data. I shall limit myself to the following arguments:

1. In Revelation we have a similar scenario where the message of the Spirit addressed to each of the seven churches of the Roman province Asia, whose capital is Ephesus, is intended for all seven churches. This is clear from the repeated injunction at the end of each address: "He who has an ear, let him hear what the Spirit says to the churches." (2:7, 11, 17, 29; 3:6, 13, 22) The universality of the one message expressed in each instance, in different words, is reflected in the numeral seven.

2. Ephesians immediately follows the letter addressed to "the (many) churches of Galatia" (Gal 1:2). I have repeatedly shown Galatians to be the blue print of the entire New Testament. It makes sense that Galatians is followed by the epistle to the Ephesians since, in Acts, Paul's last

farewell address and testament to the elders of Ephesus is aimed at the leaders of "the (one) church of God" everywhere: "Take heed to yourselves and to all the flock, in which the Holy Spirit has made you overseers, to care for the church of God which he obtained with the blood of his own Son. I know that after my departure fierce wolves will come in among you, not sparing the flock." (Acts 20:28-29)

3. The reference to the church as flock—and no less than twice in a row—is unique to Acts as well as the Pauline epistles.[1] This strikingly corresponds to the apparently unwarranted addition in Ephesians of "pastors" (*poimenes*, shepherds) before "teachers" to the established triad of gifts—"apostles, prophets, teachers"—of 1 Corinthians (12:28) in conjunction with the building of the body of Christ (v.27): "And his gifts were that some should be apostles, some prophets, some evangelists, some pastors and teachers, to equip the saints for the work of ministry, for building up the body of Christ." (Eph 4:11-12)

4. Another close link between Acts 20 and Ephesians 4 is supported by the mention of "evangelists" (*evangelistas*) (4:11), which corresponds to the reference to the "gospel" (*evangelion*) in the same context in Acts: "But I do not account my life of any value nor as precious to myself, if only I may accomplish my course and the ministry which I received from the Lord Jesus,

---

[1] The only apparent exception is found in 1 Cor 9:7 where, however, it is part of a series of examples aimed at bolstering Paul's argument for his right to be "fed" by those whom he serves: "Who serves as a soldier at his own expense? Who plants a vineyard without eating any of its fruit? Who tends a flock without getting some of the milk?"

to testify to the gospel (*evangelion*) of the grace of God." (20:24) The link is sealed through the express reference to Paul as "prisoner" (*desmios*; chained) in, on the one hand, Acts 23:18; 25:14, 27 and, on the other hand, twice in a row in Ephesians (3:1; 4:1), the only instances of such in Paul's letters to churches.[2]

Anyone familiar with the Pauline letters will readily notice that they repeatedly cover the same basic topics since Paul's "gospel" is always one and the same: "I am astonished that you are so quickly deserting him who called you in the grace of Christ and turning to a different gospel, not that there is another gospel, but there are some who trouble you and want to pervert the gospel of Christ." (Gal 1:6-7) Also noticeable is the fact that the specific content of each letter is aimed at the literary addressees of each letter. Romans revolves around the Law and its righteousness since Rome prided itself on its legal system. The Corinthian correspondence is aimed against the false wisdom of the Greeks. Galatians obliquely refers Paul's dream at the end of Romans that his gospel would reach beyond Rome to the westernmost confines of the Roman empire (15:24, 29). The area of Galatia was so named after the Gauls who had previously relocated from the west into the area of central Asia Minor and became its ruling class.[3]

The four major epistles at the head of the Pauline corpus practically cover the entire Roman empire in Europe, that is, the entire land of the Gentile Greco-Romans. These letters convey the same message that originated in Ephesus. The Pauline school purposely chose Ephesus as its capital due to its location in the

---

[2] In Philippians and Colossians we hear of Paul's "chains" (*desmois* [Phil 1:7, 14, 17]; *desmous* [Phil 1:13]; *desmōn* [Col 4:18]) but not that he is *desmios*.

[3] See my article "Paul's Letter to the Churches of Galatia," The Journal of the Orthodox Center for the Advancement of Biblical Studies (JOCABS) Vol. 9, No 1 (2016).

westernmost area of the East, the land of scripture. Ephesus, at the shore of the Greco-Roman sea facing West, was inviting the Greco-Romans into the new city of God (Rev 21:2) for their own healing.[4] Thus Ephesians is the compendium of the Pauline gospel addressed to the entire universe, East as well as West:

> Therefore remember that at one time you Gentiles in the flesh, called the uncircumcision by what is called the circumcision, which is made in the flesh by hands—remember that you were at that time separated from Christ, alienated from the commonwealth of Israel, and strangers to the covenants of promise, having no hope and without God in the world. But now in Christ Jesus you who once were far off have been brought near in the blood of Christ. For he is our peace, who has made us both one, and has broken down the dividing wall of hostility, by abolishing in his flesh the law of commandments and ordinances, that he might create in himself one new man in place of the two, so making peace, and might reconcile us both to God in one body through the cross, thereby bringing the hostility to an end. And he came and preached peace to you who were far off and peace to those who were near; for through him we both have access in one Spirit to the Father. So then you are no longer strangers and sojourners, but you are fellow citizens with the saints and members of the household of God, built upon the foundation of the apostles and prophets, Christ Jesus himself being the cornerstone, in whom the whole structure is joined together and grows into a holy temple in the Lord; in whom you also are built into it for a dwelling place of God in the Spirit. (Eph 2:11-22)

The four letters completing the Pauline diptych centered round Ephesians are ingeniously conceived. The first two, Philippians and Colossians, are clearly intended to be part of the orbit of Ephesians both formally and materially. On the one hand, they are locked into a literary unit with Ephesians through Paul's signature at the close of Colossians: "I, Paul, write this greeting with my own hand." (Col 4:18a) On the other hand, they are the only letters addressed to churches that present Paul "in chains."[5]

---

[4] See *The Rise of Scripture*, 353-6.

[5] Eph 3:1; 4:1; Phil 1:7, 13, 14, 17; Col 4:18. These church letters, along with the letter to Philemon, are referred to in scholarly circles as the "Captivity Epistles."

This feature is bluntly stressed in its conclusion to the entire trilogy after the signature: "Remember my fetters (*desmōn*; chains). Grace be with you." (Col 4:18b) Any first time reader will immediately notice that all three messages revolve around Jesus Christ being the medium through whom God brought about his plan of salvation for both Jews and Gentiles. Still one may raise the question as to why Philippi and Colossae were specifically chosen as recipients of Paul's missive. I believe that both cities function as a stand-in for Rome, that is, as a mini-Rome, so to speak, and thus correspond to Rome. Philippi was a "Roman colony" (Acts 16:12) that lay on the famous Roman road *Via Egnatia* linking Macedonia to Rome. Colossae brings to mind the Greek noun *kolossos* referring to a statue of huge proportions[6] and thus reflecting extreme power similar to that of the imperial city. More important though is their respective locations. Philippi lies in Europe, that is, in the West, whereas Colossae is a city of the Roman province Asia in the East. Still the ingeniousness lies in how the authors integrated the gospel of "submission" (*hypakoē*; [submissive] obedience) addressed to Rome (Rom 1:5; 16:26) into these two letters by belittling the empire's capital in two different ways, each befitting the addressed city. Philippi, the city conquered by the Romans is praised as the locale of the "beginning" of the gospel (Phil 4:15a; see also Acts 16:9-15), while the Romans of Rome were still on the horizon in Paul's purview, and his visit to Rome was relegated to an iffy future (Rom 15:22-29). Paul singled out the Philippians in that "no church entered into partnership with me in giving and receiving except you only" (Phil 4:15b). The belittling of Rome in Colossians is more subtle and thus more effective. One cannot help but notice that the content of that letter is a condensed form of Ephesians, four chapters compared to six. The most striking example is the house rules: 9 verses (Col 3:19-4:1) compared to 22 (Eph 5:21-6:9). It is as though Colossae, the mini-Rome, is asked to hear also Ephesians as Paul will soon require at the end of Colossians itself:

---

[6] Hence our adjective "colossal."

"Give my greetings to the brethren at Laodicea, and to Nympha and the church in her house. And when this letter has been read among you, have it read also in the church of the Laodiceans; and see that you read also the letter from Laodicea." (4:15-16) It is abundantly clear that, given the size of the two letters, the Colossians would benefit more than the Ephesians would in that exchange. In other words, scripturally speaking, the Pauline capital city Ephesus is referential for the imperial capital Rome and not vice versa.

My statement concerning the "presumed" letter to the Laodiceans as pointing to the one Paul wrote to the Ephesians sounds like an unwarranted "leap." But in the reality of the literary nature of the New Testament scripture that has been produced by the Pauline school, the hearers are constantly required to be alert to the interconnections between the different books. Since we do not have a letter to the Laodiceans in the Pauline corpus, the author is, in all probability, referring to that found in the Book of Revelation as one among seven letters addressed to seven churches of the Roman province Asia (Rev 2-3) whose capital Ephesus was the recipient of the first among the seven letters (1:1-11). At the other end of the spectrum we hear of Laodicea as being the recipient of the last letter (3:14-22). However—and this is the major point—each of the seven letters is addressed to all the other churches: "He who has an ear, let him hear what the Spirit says to *the churches.*" (2:7, 11, 17, 29; 3:6, 13, 22) Given that Colossae was also a city of the same province Asia, the hearers—addressed in 1:3—can safely conclude that the directive at the end of it to exchange "letters" between neighboring churches is meant to be a general rule.[7] Add to this that we hear specifically of one member of that community, Nympha, together with "the church in her house" (*tēn kat' oikon avtēs ekklēsian*) (Col 4:15). Nympha, meaning "bride," is a classic metaphor used to speak of the church in the

---

[7] See *C-Col* 95-106 where I have even shown that the entire passage Col 4:7-18 is intended to establish a New Testament "canon" that would encompass not only the Pauline epistles but also the entire New Testament including the Gospels through the mention of Mark and Luke.

Pauline corpus (2 Cor 11:2; Eph 5:25-32; see also 1 Cor 5:15-18). It is arguably an oblique reference to the church of Ephesus, the Pauline headquarters, especially that it is precisely in the letter to the Ephesians—immediately preceding that to the Colossians—that the church is unequivocally presented as Christ's "bride" (Eph 5:22-33).

The final two letters addressed to the city of Thessalonica serve multiple purposes as is befitting the closure of the "canon" of Paul's nine letters to churches. By splitting the short correspondence over two letters the authors intended to "honor" Alexander's homeland, Macedonia (whose capital was Thessalonica) equally with Greece (Achaia, whose capital was Corinth), the land of wisdom that Alexander conquered while spreading its wisdom to the East through his conquests.[8] Alexander and his followers, whose policies gave rise to the Old Testament writings, were dubbed as Greeks (*Hellēnes*) rather than Macedonians in scripture. Alexander was never forgotten in the purview of the New Testament and its gospel. This can be gathered from the five instances of the name Alexander in the New Testament, especially in Mark where he is put on a par with the typically Roman name Rufus:

> And they compelled a passer-by, Simon of Cyrene, who was coming in from the country, the father of Alexander and Rufus, to carry his cross. (Mk 15:21)

> On the morrow their rulers and elders and scribes were gathered together in Jerusalem, with Annas the high priest and Caiaphas and John and Alexander, and all who were of the high-priestly family. (Acts 4:5-6)

> Some of the crowd prompted Alexander, whom the Jews had put forward. And Alexander motioned with his hand, wishing to make a defense to the people. (Acts 19:33)

---

[8] My readers are reminded that Alexander was Aristotle's pupil.

By rejecting conscience, certain persons have made shipwreck of their faith, among them Hymenaeus and Alexander, whom I have delivered to Satan that they may learn not to blaspheme. (1Tim 1:19-20)

Alexander the coppersmith did me great harm; the Lord will requite him for his deeds. (2Tim 4:14)

Thus, Macedonia was hardly an afterthought. It is referred to in Romans as having responded, together with Achaia, to Paul's appeal to help him realize the commitment he made at the Jerusalem meeting to "remember the poor" (Gal 2:10): "For Macedonia and Achaia have been pleased to make some contribution for the poor among the saints at Jerusalem." (Rom 15:26) Notice how Macedonia is given precedence over Achaia. That such precedence is intentional is apparent from the last chapter of 1 Corinthians:

On the first day of every week, each of you is to put something aside and store it up, as he may prosper, so that contributions need not be made when I come. And when I arrive, I will send those whom you accredit by letter to carry your gift to Jerusalem. If it seems advisable that I should go also, they will accompany me. I will visit you after passing through Macedonia, for I intend to pass through Macedonia, and perhaps I will stay with you or even spend the winter, so that you may speed me on my journey, wherever I go. (1Cor 16:2-6)

And as if this were not enough, Alexander's Macedonia is given importance in the second letter addressed to those in Corinth, Achaia's capital city, by referring to it no less than seven times throughout the letter (2 Cor 1:16 [twice]; 2:13; 7:5; 8:1; 9:2; 11:9). Given this seemingly unnecessary mention of Macedonia in an address to Corinth, it prepares the Corinthians to hear, at some point, the correspondence aimed at Thessalonica, i.e., they are being programmed to expect that Thessalonica be honored with some attention from Paul's pen. Instead of a modicum of attention, Thessalonica is honored with two letters, just as was Corinth. What is nevertheless striking is the flagrant deliberateness of this matter. Both letters to the Thessalonians amount to eight chapters, that is, to half the size of 1 Corinthians (16 chapters) and two-thirds the size of 2 Corinthians (13).[9]

As for the size of the letters to the Thessalonians, it is understandable in view of the fact that Ephesians has already summed up the teaching of Romans and 1 and 2 Corinthians, a summation repeated twice, once in Philippians and once in Colossians.[10] The threefold summary is a well-attested scriptural device: the numeral three reflects the "indeed-ness" of the matter in the same way "thrice holy" seals the utter holiness of the referent.[11] The question that remains to be answered is whether the Thessalonian correspondence sounds like a boring tail end rehashing of the summation or whether it carries it a step further. In order to find a plausible, if not convincing answer, one should compare the contents of the last five epistles.

Ephesians subsumes the message of Paul's gospel detailed in the first four letters, which was masterfully condensed in a nutshell in Galatians, the blue print of the entire New Testament:

For through the Spirit, by faith, we wait for the *hope* of righteousness. For in Christ Jesus neither circumcision nor uncircumcision is of any avail, but *faith* working through *love*. (5:5-6)

Compare this with the beginning of Ephesians:

He [God] destined us in love to be his sons through Jesus Christ, according to the purpose of his will, to the praise of his glorious grace which he freely bestowed on us in the Beloved ... In him [Christ], according to the purpose of him who accomplishes all

---

[9] This is not counting that the average size of the chapters of these two letters is longer than the average of same in the Thessalonian correspondence.

[10] See above on the clustering of these three letters compared to that of the rest of the corpus of Paul's epistles to churches.

[11] See my Excursus on Number Symbolism in *NTI₄* 22-28.

things according to the counsel of his will, we who first *hoped* in Christ have been destined and appointed to live for the praise of his glory. In him you also, who have heard *the word of truth, the gospel of your salvation*,[12] and have *believed*[13] in him, were sealed with the promised Holy Spirit, which is the guarantee of our inheritance until we acquire possession of it, to the praise of his glory. For this reason, because I have heard of your *faith* in the Lord Jesus and your *love* toward all the saints, I do not cease to give thanks for you, remembering you in my prayers, that the God of our Lord Jesus Christ, the Father of glory, may give you a spirit of wisdom and of revelation in the knowledge of him, having the eyes of your hearts enlightened, that you may know what is the *hope* to which he has called you, what are the riches of his glorious inheritance in the saints. (1:5-6, 11-18)

In both Galatians and Ephesians the triad of faith, love, and hope are functional in the following sequence: faith (trust) is necessarily expressed in love, and both are be sustained in hope that one may reach the end of the road. In other words, not only faith is conditional on love, but both faith and love are conditional on hope, since the end has not come yet. The novelty in the language of Ephesians makes it clear that faith and love have different recipients. The trust (faith) is directed toward God and his Christ, while love is directed toward our peers. The entire message is revisited in both Philippians and Colossians. In Philippians the message is both expanded and detailed, especially in regard to the "end" which is always ahead and not yet here.[14] In Colossians, the third captivity letter, it is expectedly succinctly and masterfully put:

And I am sure that he who began a good work in you will bring it to completion at the day of Jesus Christ … And it is my prayer that your *love* may abound more and more, with knowledge and all discernment, so that you may approve what is excellent, and may

---

[12] The reference to the Pauline preaching as the word of truth and the gospel harks back to Galatians.

[13] In Greek the noun "faith" (*pistis*) and the verb "believe" (*pistevo*) are from the same root *pist—*.

[14] See below my comments on this matter in conjunction with the Thessalonian correspondence.

be pure and blameless for the day of Christ … Convinced of this, I know that I shall remain and continue with you all, for your progress and joy in the *faith* … Only let your manner of life be worthy of *the gospel of Christ*, so that whether I come and see you or am absent, I may hear of you that you stand firm in one spirit, with one mind striving side by side for *the faith of the gospel*, and not frightened in anything by your opponents (*antikeimenōn*).[15] (Phil 1:6, 9-10, 25, 27-28)

We always thank God, the Father of our Lord Jesus Christ, when we pray for you, because we have heard of *your faith in Christ Jesus* and of *the love which you have for all the saints*, because of *the hope laid up for you in heaven*. Of this you have heard before in *the word of the truth, the gospel*. (Col 1:3-5)

At this point one cannot help but notice that the concise rendering in Colossians corresponds to what we heard in Galatians 5:5-6, especially that both these letters were literarily conceived with a "broader" audience in mind. Galatians is addressed to many churches (1:2) whereas Colossians ends with the following injunction: "And when this letter has been read among you, have it read also in the church of the Laodiceans; and see that you read also the letter from Laodicea." (4:16)

Now that the Pauline "gospel of God" to the Romans (Rom 1:1) has been encapsulated in the letter to Colossae, mini-Rome, the Pauline school extends its message specifically to the land of Alexander, the promoter of Hellenism, so that Alexander's followers in Macedonia would join those of his "brother" Rufus (a stand-in for Rome) in accepting the invitation to "carry Jesus'— and their own[16]—cross" (Mk 15:21). The important aspects of faith, love and hope, are emphasized throughout the Pauline writings, particularly in Romans and 1 and 2 Corinthians, and are immediately and repeatedly stressed in 1 and 2 Thessalonians:

---

[15] See my comments below in conjunction with 2 Thessalonians.

[16] See my comments in *NTI₁* 227, fn 12.

We give thanks to God always for you all, constantly mentioning you in our prayers, remembering before our God and Father your work of *faith* and labor of *love* and *steadfastness of hope* in our Lord Jesus Christ. (1 Thess 1:2-3)

We are bound to give thanks to God always for you, brethren, as is fitting, because your *faith* is growing abundantly, and the *love* of every one of you for one another is increasing. Therefore we ourselves boast of you in the churches of God for your *steadfastness*[17] and *faith* in all your persecutions and in the afflictions which you are enduring. (2 Thess 1:3-4)

The ending of 1 Thessalonians rejoins the ending of Ephesians by referencing Isaiah 59:17,[18] making the latter letter in the canon seem to be a copy of the former:

Stand therefore, having girded your loins with truth, and having put on the breastplate of righteousness, and having shod your feet with the equipment of the gospel of peace; besides all these, taking the shield of faith, with which you can quench all the flaming darts of the evil one. And take the helmet of salvation, and the sword of the Spirit, which is the word of God. (Eph 6:14-17)

But, since we belong to the day, let us be sober, and put on the breastplate of faith and love, and for a helmet the hope of salvation. For God has not destined us for wrath, but to obtain salvation through our Lord Jesus Christ. (1 Thess 5:8-9)

However, the more important input of the Thessalonian correspondence is to keep in check the misunderstanding that hope is equal to guaranteed assuredness of the promised end, no matter what. That is why at the end of 1 Thessalonians, just as Paul unequivocally stated in 1 Corinthians 15, one hears of the coming of Jesus—and our joining him through our being raised—as a future, and not already consummated, event:

---

[17] Steadfastness is the other side of the coin of hope (1 Thess 1:3). See my comments in *1 Thess* 39.

[18] He put on righteousness as a breastplate, and a helmet of salvation upon his head; he put on garments of vengeance for clothing, and wrapped himself in fury as a mantle.

But we would not have you ignorant, brethren, concerning those who are asleep, that you may not grieve as others do who have no hope. For since we believe that Jesus died and rose again, even so, through Jesus, God will bring with him those who have fallen asleep. For this we declare to you by the word of the Lord, that we who are alive, who are left until the coming of the Lord, shall not precede those who have fallen asleep. For the Lord himself will descend from heaven with a cry of command, with the archangel's call, and with the sound of the trumpet of God. And the dead in Christ will rise first; then we who are alive, who are left, shall be caught up together with them in the clouds to meet the Lord in the air; and so we shall always be with the Lord. Therefore comfort one another with these words. (1 Thess 4:13-18)

What the believers are summoned to do in the meantime is to walk the way, as Paul made abundantly clear earlier in Romans:

But if we have died with Christ, we believe that we shall also live with him. For we know that Christ being raised from the dead will never die again; death no longer has dominion over him. The death he died he died to sin, once for all, but the life he lives he lives to God. So you also must consider yourselves dead to sin and alive to God in Christ Jesus. Let not sin therefore reign in your mortal bodies, to make you obey their passions. Do not yield your members to sin as instruments of wickedness, but yield yourselves to God as men who have been brought from death to life, and your members to God as instruments of righteousness. For sin will have no dominion over you, since you are not under law but under grace. What then? Are we to sin because we are not under law but under grace? By no means! (Rom 6:8-15)

But as to the times and the seasons, brethren, you have no need to have anything written to you. For you yourselves know well that the day of the Lord will come like a thief in the night. When people say, "There is peace and security," then sudden destruction will come upon them as travail comes upon a woman with child, and there will be no escape. But you are not in darkness, brethren, for that day to surprise you like a thief. For you are all sons of light and sons of the day; we are not of the night or of darkness. So then let us not sleep, as others do, but let us keep awake and be sober. For those who sleep sleep at night, and those who get drunk are drunk at night. But, since we belong to the day, let us be sober, and put on the breastplate of faith and love, and for a helmet the hope of salvation. (1 Thess 5:1-8)

Eternal life is not an already given, but always lies ahead only for those who will have walked the way as "saints": "But then what return did you get from the things of which you are now ashamed? The end of those things is death. But now that you have been set free from sin and have become slaves of God, the return you get is sanctification and its end, eternal life." (Rom 6:21-22)[19]

The importance of this aspect of the teaching was so crucial that it is repeated in an extreme fashion in 2 Thessalonians. This letter is essentially a literary construct that assumes that the hearers of 1 Thessalonians did not heed the message of its chapters 4 and 5, and needed to hear unequivocally that "the Lord has not come yet":

> Now concerning the coming of our Lord Jesus Christ and our assembling to meet him, we beg you, brethren, not to be quickly shaken in mind or excited, either by spirit or by word, or by letter purporting to be from us, to the effect that the day of the Lord has come. Let no one deceive you in any way; for that day will not come, unless the rebellion comes first, and the man of lawlessness is revealed, the son of perdition, who opposes (*antikeimenos*) and exalts himself against every so-called god or object of worship, so that he takes his seat in the temple of God, proclaiming himself to be God. (2 Thess 2:1-4)

One cannot miss that *antikeimenos*, which is very rare in the New Testament, harks back to the opponents (*antikeimenōn*) of Philippians 1:28 who are trying to derail the believers on their last stretch toward the coming kingdom. In other words, Satan works through his representative as Paul already underscored in 2

---

[19] See my comments in *C-Rom* 123-4.

Corinthians 11:13-15.[20] This linkage is sealed in that the third and only other instance of "opponents" occurs in 1 Corinthians 16:9, that is, a few verses after Paul's extensive dealing with the resurrection in the previous chapter and, no less, in conjunction with his stay in Ephesus whose citizens were the recipients of Ephesians: "But I will stay in Ephesus until Pentecost, for a wide door for effective work has opened to me, and there are many adversaries (*antikeimenoi*)." (1 Cor 16:8-9)

---

[20] For such men are false apostles, deceitful workmen, disguising themselves as apostles of Christ. And no wonder, for even Satan disguises himself as an angel of light. So it is not strange if his servants also disguise themselves as servants of righteousness. Their end will correspond to their deeds.

Chapter 1

Vv. 1:14 ¹Παῦλος ἀπόστολος Χριστοῦ Ἰησοῦ διὰ θελήματος θεοῦ τοῖς ἁγίοις τοῖς οὖσιν ἔν Ἐφέσῳ καὶ πιστοῖς ἐν Χριστῷ Ἰησοῦ ²χάρις ὑμῖν καὶ εἰρήνη ἀπὸ θεοῦ πατρὸς ἡμῶν καὶ κυρίου Ἰησοῦ Χριστοῦ ³Εὐλογητὸς ὁ θεὸς καὶ πατὴρ τοῦ κυρίου ἡμῶν Ἰησοῦ Χριστοῦ ὁ εὐλογήσας ἡμᾶς ἐν πάσῃ εὐλογίᾳ πνευματικῇ ἐν τοῖς ἐπουρανίοις ἐν Χριστῷ ⁴καθὼς ἐξελέξατο ἡμᾶς ἐν αὐτῷ πρὸ καταβολῆς κόσμου εἶναι ἡμᾶς ἁγίους καὶ ἀμώμους κατενώπιον αὐτοῦ ἐν ἀγάπῃ ⁵προορίσας ἡμᾶς εἰς υἱοθεσίαν διὰ Ἰησοῦ Χριστοῦ εἰς αὐτόν κατὰ τὴν εὐδοκίαν τοῦ θελήματος αὐτοῦ ⁶εἰς ἔπαινον δόξης τῆς χάριτος αὐτοῦ ἧς ἐχαρίτωσεν ἡμᾶς ἐν τῷ ἠγαπημένῳ ⁷Ἐν ᾧ ἔχομεν τὴν ἀπολύτρωσιν διὰ τοῦ αἵματος αὐτοῦ τὴν ἄφεσιν τῶν παραπτωμάτων κατὰ τὸ πλοῦτος τῆς χάριτος αὐτοῦ ⁸ἧς ἐπερίσσευσεν εἰς ἡμᾶς ἐν πάσῃ σοφίᾳ καὶ φρονήσει ⁹γνωρίσας ἡμῖν τὸ μυστήριον τοῦ θελήματος αὐτοῦ κατὰ τὴν εὐδοκίαν αὐτοῦ ἦν προέθετο ἐν αὐτῷ ¹⁰εἰς οἰκονομίαν τοῦ πληρώματος τῶν καιρῶν ἀνακεφαλαιώσασθαι τὰ πάντα ἐν τῷ Χριστῷ τὰ ἐπὶ τοῖς οὐρανοῖς καὶ τὰ ἐπὶ τῆς γῆς ἐν αὐτῷ ¹¹Ἐν ᾧ καὶ ἐκληρώθημεν προορισθέντες κατὰ πρόθεσιν τοῦ τὰ πάντα ἐνεργοῦντος κατὰ τὴν βουλὴν τοῦ θελήματος αὐτοῦ ¹²εἰς τὸ εἶναι ἡμᾶς εἰς ἔπαινον δόξης αὐτοῦ τοὺς προηλπικότας ἐν τῷ Χριστῷ ¹³ Ἐν ᾧ καὶ ὑμεῖς ἀκούσαντες τὸν λόγον τῆς ἀληθείας τὸ εὐαγγέλιον τῆς σωτηρίας ὑμῶν ἐν ᾧ καὶ πιστεύσαντες ἐσφραγίσθητε τῷ πνεύματι τῆς ἐπαγγελίας τῷ ἁγίῳ ¹⁴ὅ ἐστιν ἀρραβὼν τῆς κληρονομίας ἡμῶν εἰς ἀπολύτρωσιν τῆς περιποιήσεως εἰς ἔπαινον τῆς δόξης αὐτοῦ

¹Paul, an apostle of Christ Jesus by the will of God, To the saints who are also faithful in Christ Jesus: ²Grace to you and peace from God our Father and the Lord Jesus Christ. ³Blessed be the God and Father of our Lord Jesus Christ, who has blessed us in Christ with every spiritual

41

blessing in the heavenly places, ⁴even as he chose us in him before the foundation of the world, that we should be holy and blameless before him. ⁵He destined us in love to be his sons through Jesus Christ, according to the purpose of his will, ⁶to the praise of his glorious grace which he freely bestowed on us in the Beloved. ⁷In him we have redemption through his blood, the forgiveness of our trespasses, according to the riches of his grace ⁸which he lavished upon us. ⁹For he has made known to us in all wisdom and insight the mystery of his will, according to his purpose which he set forth in Christ ¹⁰as a plan for the fulness of time, to unite all things in him, things in heaven and things on earth. ¹¹In him, according to the purpose of him who accomplishes all things according to the counsel of his will, ¹²we who first hoped in Christ have been destined and appointed to live for the praise of his glory.¹³In him you also, who have heard the word of truth, the gospel of your salvation, and have believed in him, were sealed with the promised Holy Spirit, ¹⁴which is the guarantee of our inheritance until we acquire possession of it, to the praise of his glory.

A quick overview of Ephesians will show that it follows, in a story like manner, the basic message of Galatians. The "story" describes how the Law, which was handed down to the scriptural Israel (chapter 1), yet aimed also at the scriptural Gentiles[1] (chapter 2), reached the Gentiles through Paul's preaching (chapter 3). Then, before engaging in the general rules for the new way of life (4:17-5:20)—and therein lies the masterful twist since it sounds as an aside—Paul brings into the picture the metaphor of the one body (4:1-16), which was dealt with in the first major epistles (Rom 12; 1 Cor 12). This twist was subtly

---

[1]And all Israel, *sojourner* as well as homeborn, with their elders and officers and their judges, stood on opposite sides of the ark before the Levitical priests who carried the ark of the covenant of the Lord, half of them in front of Mount Gerizim and half of them in front of Mount Ebal, as Moses the servant of the Lord had commanded at the first, that they should bless the people of Israel. And afterward he read all the words of the law, the blessing and the curse, according to all that is written in the book of the law. There was not a word of all that Moses commanded which Joshua did not read before all the assembly of Israel, and the women, and the little ones, *and the sojourners who lived among them.* (Josh 8:33-35)

prepared for in Ephesians 2:11-22 where he spoke of the one building[2] made of both Jews and Gentiles. Then he proceeds along the lines of 1 Corinthians 14 zeroing in on the actual socio-political setting of *his house churches*, that is, the Roman household (Eph 5:21-6:9). Finally, he ends by reminding his addressees that they are to tread the path that still lies ahead (6:10-20), since the Lord has not yet come. This, in turn, sets the tone for the Thessalonian correspondence.

The major blunder of classical theology is to hear the New Testament with a Platonic mind: in other words, everything that has to do with God and the church is conceived along Platonic lines, and then such thinking is poured into those two terms frequently used by Paul. Even Jesus who was a "human being" (*anthrōpos*; 1 Tim 2:5) is cast as a preexistent eternal entity that "entered into our world."[3] A classic example of this theology is seen in the handling of Galatians 4:5 (But when the time had fully come, God sent forth his Son, born of woman, born under the law) where the preexistence of the Son is simply assumed through references to other passages in the New Testament extraneous to Galatians.[4] No serious exegete can possibly deduce such from the narrative and argument of Galatians itself. Platonic thinking, however, became part and parcel of "theological" exegesis, which amounts to plain eisegesis. What compels me to bring up this point here is that Ephesians 1:3-14 presents us with a conundrum due to its recurring use of the preposition *pro* (before):

> even as he [God] chose us in him before (*pro*) the foundation of the world, that we should be holy and blameless before him. He destined (*proorisas*) us in love to be his sons through Jesus Christ, according to the purpose of his will. (vv.4-5 RSV)

> According as he hath chosen us in him before (*pro*) the foundation of the world, that we should be holy and without blame before him in love: Having predestinated (*proorisas*) us unto the adoption of

---

[2] As in 1 Cor 3:9-17.
[3] Through a virgin who remained a virgin.
[4] See my comments on this verse in Gal 201-6.

children by Jesus Christ to himself, according to the good pleasure of his will. (vv.4-5 KJV)

For he has made known to us in all wisdom and insight the mystery of his will, according to his purpose which he set forth (*proetheto*; set beforehand) in Christ. (v.9 RSV)

Having made known unto us the mystery of his will, according to his good pleasure which he hath purposed (*proetheto*; set beforehand) in himself. (v.9 KJV)

In him, according to the purpose (*prothesin*) of him who accomplishes all things according to the counsel of his will, we who first hoped (*proēlpikotas*) in Christ have been destined (*prooristhentes*) and appointed to live for the praise of his glory. (vv.11-12 RSV)

In whom also we have obtained an inheritance, being predestinated (*prooristhentes*) according to the purpose (*prothesin*) of him who worketh all things after the counsel of his own will: That we should be to the praise of his glory, who first trusted (*proēlpikotas*) in Christ. (vv.11-12 KJV)

Even without realizing it, theologians start with "before the foundation of the world" on which they base their philosophical "eternal" approach, and then "conclude" that the entire passage (Eph 1:3-14) is referring to a plan God had in mind "before" he created the world. And since Christ is the main object or content of his plan, then he must be eternal. Understanding *pro katabolēs kosmou* in this sense is preposterous for a number of reasons.

First of all, it is the phrase *apo katabolēs kosmou* (from the foundation of the world) that is commonly encountered in the New Testament (Mt 13:35; 25:34; Lk 11:50; Heb 4:3; 9:25; Rev 13:8; 17:8). Two exceptions are John 17:24 and 1 Peter 1:20. The latter is interesting for our case in that (1) it appears in conjunction with the use of another *pro* in the same context and (2) the vein of thought parallels that in Ephesians: "He [Christ] was destined (**pro**egnōsmenou; **fore**ordained KJV) before (*pro*) the foundation of the world but was made manifest at the end of the times for your sake." (1 Pet 1:20) As for John, I am convinced the usage has to do with the reference to God's love which is central in that gospel[5] and is the main point in Ephesians 1:4. So *pro katabolēs kosmou* is to be taken as a literary hyperbolic case of *apo katabolēs kosmou* in order to underscore that God's love takes precedence over anything else in dealing with us and, more importantly, it is not triggered by something else as though it were a response or a reaction on God's part. The same concern is found elsewhere in the New Testament, the most striking example being the way the matter is handled in 1 John: "We love, because he first loved us" (4:19).[6]

Secondly, and more to the point, taking *pro* literally as meaning "before" the foundation of the world and thus referring to a philosophically understood eternity does not make sense in the case of *hēmas... tous proēlpikotas* (us... who have beforehand hoped) in Ephesians 1:12. Notice how the translations tend to eschew the difficulty by taking the *pro* in this case as meaning "first" compared to others:

> we who first hoped in Christ have been destined and appointed to live for the praise of his glory (RSV)

> That we should be to the praise of his glory, who first trusted in Christ (KJV)

> to the end that we should be unto the praise of his glory, we who had *before* hoped in Christ (ASV)

> so that we who were the first to hope in Christ might be to the praise of his glory (ESV)

---

[5] See especially Jn 3:16: "For God so loved the world that he gave his only Son, that whoever believes in him should not perish but have eternal life." Notice the parallelism in content with Eph 1:4.

[6] The original is more forceful. The reason is that the English could be taken as an adverb referring to the action of loving, whereas the Greek is unequivocal in that *prōtos* (first) is a masculine adjective referring clearly to God as being (the) first, in order, to do so. The result is that when we love, we are at best second in line, someone already beat us to it.

to the end that we who were the first to hope in Christ should be
to the praise of His glory (NAS)

What is compelling is that all of these translations are in agreement
that "first" is the only possible rendition of the original. In other
words, the statement in this verse is to be heard from the
perspective of the scriptural Israel. There is no need to enter into
whether the "we" in this verse is inclusive of the Gentiles or
applies only to the Jews. The Jews are never in the literary purview
of the author given that the term "Jew" is nowhere to be found in
Ephesians.[7] Although uncircumcision versus circumcision is
mentioned in Ephesians 3:11, it is the term "Gentiles" that occurs
profusely (2:11; 3:1, 6, 8; 4:17) throughout the letter. What is
important is that the element hope is an essential part of the
statement concerning both parties:

> Therefore remember that at one time you Gentiles in the flesh,
> called the uncircumcision by what is called the circumcision, which
> is made in the flesh by hands—remember that you were at that time
> separated from Christ, alienated from the commonwealth of Israel,
> and strangers to the covenants of promise, having no hope and
> without God in the world. (2:11-12)

Notice further how the two are unified under the title "the
commonwealth of Israel" into which the Gentiles are integrated.
Thus, the conclusion is unavoidable: the entire perspective of
Ephesians 1:3-14 is that of the Old Testament writings and,
consequently, it is to be heard accordingly. The intensive usage of
pro draws Paul's Gentile hearers into the world of the Old
Testament where one hears of God's "managed plan" (*oikonomia*):
"For he has made known to us in all wisdom and insight the
mystery of his will, according to his purpose which he set forth in
Christ as a plan (*oikonomian*) for the fulness of time, to unite all
things in him, things in heaven and things on earth." (vv.9-10)
When one recalls that *oikonomia* is precisely the term Paul uses to

---

[7] This is striking, the least to say, since it appears in the clone letter Colossians (3:11).

refer to his apostleship,[8] then one cannot but conclude that Ephesians 1:3-14 is written from the perspective of "the (Pauline) word of truth, the gospel of your salvation" (v.13) with which the author concludes the entire passage after having used *pro* three times in a row (vv.11-12) and, no less, following his referring to *oikonomian* (v.10).

Last and in no way least is the rare use of the verb *anakephalaiōsasthai* in 1:10 (which is translated as diversely as "unite" [RSV; ESV], "gather together" [KJV], "sum[ming] up" [ASV; NAS]), that inevitably brings to mind the only other time it is used in the New Testament: "Owe no one anything, except to love one another; for he who loves his neighbor has fulfilled the law. The commandments, 'You shall not commit adultery, You shall not kill, You shall not steal, You shall not covet,' and any other commandment, are summed up (*anakephalaioutai*) in this sentence, 'You shall love your neighbor as yourself.'" (Rom 13:8-9) One cannot escape the distinct impression that the presentation of the Old Testament in Ephesians is the foretelling of God's plan to include the uncircumcised in the commonwealth of the scriptural Israel under the aegis of God's law. This the basis for the statement in 1 John whereby the New Testament does not bring anything new, let alone over and above the Law of God:

> My little children, I am writing this to you so that you may not sin; but if any one does sin, we have an advocate with the Father, Jesus Christ the righteous; and he is the expiation for our sins, and not for ours only but also for the sins of the whole world. And by this we may be sure that we know him, if we keep his commandments. He who says "I know him" but disobeys his commandments is a liar, and the truth is not in him; but whoever keeps his word, in him truly love for God is perfected. By this we may be sure that we are in him: he who says he abides in him ought to walk in the same way in which he walked. Beloved, I am writing you no new commandment, but an old commandment which you had from the beginning; the old commandment is the word which you have

---

[8] For if I do this of my own will, I have a reward; but if not of my own will, I am entrusted with a commission (*oikonomian*). (1 Cor 9:17)

heard. Yet I am writing you a new commandment, which is true in him and in you, because the darkness is passing away and the true light is already shining. He who says he is in the light and hates his brother is in the darkness still. He who loves his brother abides in the light, and in it there is no cause for stumbling. But he who hates his brother is in the darkness and walks in the darkness, and does not know where he is going, because the darkness has blinded his eyes. (2:1-11)[9]

Still, as I indicated in the Introduction, the Pauline corpus was conceived as a whole that was tightly knit together through a similar "signature" at the end of each cluster. Looking more closely at the matter, one discovers that the clustering is highly artificial and thus intentional. The first instance of the Pauline signature is found at the end of 1 Corinthians, thus splitting two letters to the same community. This is strange in view of the following: (1) Romans could have been clustered with Galatians, especially in that they are close in content and this would allow the Corinthian correspondence to form a unit; (2) both letters to the Thessalonians are lumped together through one signature at the end of the second letter; (3) the Captivity Epistles are linked through the reference to Paul in chains. One could surmise that the reason to arrange the letters in such a manner was to give Romans the place of honor. But even then, why not move Galatians up next to Romans or why two letters to Corinth? The way it stands, 1 and 2 Corinthians are on a straddle, so to speak, between the first and second units of the Pauline corpus. On the other hand, content wise, the message of 1 and 2 Thessalonians "follows" the one initiated in the Captivity Epistles. The end result is that the Pauline canon forces one to submit to an unusual sequential order in hearing the epistles. Since Ephesians is heard immediately after Galatians, one would expect it to be closely linked to the "law of love" that was heard merely two chapters earlier in Galatians 5:14: "For the whole law is fulfilled in one

---

[9] This goes hand in hand with what I said in *The Rise of Scripture* regarding the entire epistolary—Catholic as well as Pauline—corpus being one under the aegis of the gospel whose champion is Paul. Pp. 343-50.

word, 'You shall love your neighbor as yourself.'" A further link to Galatians can be detected in the unexpected triple stress on the idea of "blessing" at the head of Ephesians' extensive introductory words (1:3-14) in conjunction with the inclusion of the Gentiles under the hope of the scriptural Israel, thus relegating the customary opening of thanksgiving to verse 15: "Blessed be the God and Father of our Lord Jesus Christ, who has blessed us in Christ with every spiritual blessing in the heavenly places." (v.3) This importance, if not centrality, of the same blessing bestowed inclusively upon the scriptural Gentiles as well as the scriptural Israel was the culmination of Paul's first lengthy argument from scripture itself a few chapters earlier in the epistle to the Galatians (3:1-14): "Christ redeemed us from the curse of the law, having become a curse for us—for it is written, 'Cursed be every one who hangs on a tree'—that in Christ Jesus the blessing of Abraham might come upon the Gentiles, that we might receive the promise of the Spirit through faith." (vv.13-14) The "we" before "might receive" is inclusive of both Jews and Gentiles.[10]

Vv. 15:23 [15]Διὰ τοῦτο κἀγὼ ἀκούσας τὴν καθ᾽ ὑμᾶς πίστιν ἐν τῷ κυρίῳ Ἰησοῦ καὶ τὴν ἀγάπην τὴν εἰς πάντας τοὺς ἁγίους [16]οὐ παύομαι εὐχαριστῶν ὑπὲρ ὑμῶν μνείαν ποιούμενος ἐπὶ τῶν προσευχῶν μού [17]ἵνα ὁ θεὸς τοῦ κυρίου ἡμῶν Ἰησοῦ Χριστοῦ ὁ πατὴρ τῆς δόξης· δώῃ ὑμῖν πνεῦμα σοφίας καὶ ἀποκαλύψεως ἐν ἐπιγνώσει αὐτοῦ [18]πεφωτισμένους τοὺς ὀφθαλμοὺς τῆς καρδίας ᾽ὑμῶν᾽ εἰς τὸ εἰδέναι ὑμᾶς τίς ἐστιν ἡ ἐλπὶς τῆς κλήσεως αὐτοῦ τίς ὁ πλοῦτος τῆς δόξης τῆς κληρονομίας αὐτοῦ ἐν τοῖς ἁγίοις [19]καὶ τί τὸ ὑπερβάλλον μέγεθος τῆς δυνάμεως αὐτοῦ εἰς ἡμᾶς τοὺς πιστεύοντας κατὰ τὴν ἐνέργειαν τοῦ κράτους τῆς ἰσχύος αὐτοῦ [20]Ἣν ἐνήργησεν ἐν τῷ Χριστῷ ἐγείρας αὐτὸν ἐκ νεκρῶν καὶ καθίσας ἐν δεξιᾷ αὐτοῦ ἐν τοῖς ἐπουρανίοις [21]ὑπεράνω πάσης ἀρχῆς καὶ ἐξουσίας καὶ δυνάμεως καὶ κυριότητος καὶ παντὸς ὀνόματος

---

[10] See *Gal* 129-37.

50   EPHESIANS & 2 THESSALONIANS: A COMMENTARY

ὀνομαζομένου οὐ μόνον ἐν τῷ αἰῶνι τούτῳ ἀλλὰ καὶ ἐν
τῷ μέλλοντι· ²²καὶ πάντα ὑπέταξεν ὑπὸ τοὺς πόδας αὐτοῦ
καὶ αὐτὸν ἔδωκεν κεφαλὴν ὑπὲρ πάντα τῇ ἐκκλησίᾳ ²³ἥτις
ἐστὶν τὸ σῶμα αὐτοῦ τὸ πλήρωμα τοῦ τὰ πάντα ἐν πᾶσιν
πληρουμένου

¹⁵For this reason, because I have heard of your faith in the Lord Jesus
and your love toward all the saints, ¹⁶I do not cease to give thanks for
you, remembering you in my prayers, ¹⁷that the God of our Lord Jesus
Christ, the Father of glory, may give you a spirit of wisdom and of
revelation in the knowledge of him, ¹⁸having the eyes of your hearts
enlightened, that you may know what is the hope to which he has called
you, what are the riches of his glorious inheritance in the saints, ¹⁹and
what is the immeasurable greatness of his power in us who believe,
according to the working of his great might ²⁰which he accomplished in
Christ when he raised him from the dead and made him sit at his right
hand in the heavenly places, ²¹far above all rule and authority and power
and dominion, and above every name that is named, not only in this age
but also in that which is to come; ²²and he has put all things under his
feet and has made him the head over all things for the church, ²³which is
his body, the fulness of him who fills all in all.

In order to understand correctly the meaning and function of
Ephesians 1:15-23 one needs, more than ever, to desist from
starting with the Platonic premise of the eternal and make the
effort to perceive the passage with the ears and mind of the
original addresses who were living in the Roman empire of the
time. Paul was trying to make them submit to God's law in their
socio-political context. Put otherwise, they were "fleshly" (2:11)
and Paul was trying to integrate them in God's "spiritual" building
(v.22) through submission to the "lawful" dictates of that Spirit,
as he had already established at the conclusion of his blue print
letter, which for the hearers is just two chapters before Ephesians
1:

For you were called to freedom, brethren; only do not use your
freedom as an opportunity for the flesh, but through love be

servants of one another. For the whole law is fulfilled in one word, "You shall love your neighbor as yourself." But if you bite and devour one another take heed that you are not consumed by one another. But I say, walk by the Spirit, and do not gratify the desires of the flesh. For the desires of the flesh are against the Spirit, and the desires of the Spirit are against the flesh; for these are opposed to each other, to prevent you from doing what you would. But if you are led by the Spirit you are not under the law. Now the works of the flesh are plain: fornication, impurity, licentiousness, idolatry, sorcery, enmity, strife, jealousy, anger, selfishness, dissension, party spirit, envy, drunkenness, carousing, and the like. I warn you, as I warned you before, that those who do such things shall not inherit the kingdom of God. But the fruit of the Spirit is love, joy, peace, patience, kindness, goodness, faithfulness, gentleness, self-control; against such there is no law. And those who belong to Christ Jesus have crucified the flesh with its passions and desires. If we live by the Spirit, let us also walk by the Spirit. Let us have no self-conceit, no provoking of one another, no envy of one another. (Gal 5:13-26)

When keeping in mind the two referents, the Old Testament scripture and the Roman socio-polity, without appealing to mysticism that pervaded theological thought and jargon, Ephesians 1:15-23 becomes clear and readily understandable. As is evident from Romans 15:15-16 and Philippians 2:17, Paul is presented as the high priest of the Gentiles, a function asserted in Acts where he is said to be a tent maker (Acts 18:3), the tent being none other than the tent of testimony where the great priest Aaron stood before the Lord: "In the tent of meeting, outside the veil which is before the testimony, Aaron and his sons shall tend it from evening to morning before the Lord. It shall be a statute for ever to be observed throughout their generations by the people of Israel." (Ex 27:21) In the Pauline teaching, this tent is now in the heavenly Zion:

Now Hagar is Mount Sinai in Arabia; she corresponds to the present Jerusalem, for she is in slavery with her children. But the Jerusalem above is free, and she is our mother. For it is written, "Rejoice, O barren one who does not bear; break forth and shout, you who are not in travail; for the children of the desolate one are many more than the children of her that is married." (Gal 4:25-27)

After this I looked, and the temple of the tent of witness in heaven was opened, and out of the temple came the seven angels with the seven plagues, robed in pure bright linen, and their breasts girded with golden girdles. (Rev 15:5-6)

Then I saw a new heaven and a new earth; for the first heaven and the first earth had passed away, and the sea was no more. And I saw the holy city, new Jerusalem, coming down out of heaven from God, prepared as a bride adorned for her husband; and I heard a loud voice from the throne saying, "Behold, the dwelling of God is with men. He will dwell with them, and they shall be his people, and God himself will be with them; he will wipe away every tear from their eyes, and death shall be no more, neither shall there be mourning nor crying nor pain any more, for the former things have passed away." (21:1-4)

As in all his letters, Paul raises a prayer of thanksgiving to God on behalf and for the sake of the Gentiles whose apostle he is, without any need for Jerusalem and its temple. This independence from Jerusalem goes hand in hand with independence from Rome and its powerful rulers since God established his Christ as the righteous one, in spite of his condemnation by both Rome and Jerusalem, and raised him above all authority not only on earth, but also in the heavenly places (Eph 1:20; see also Phil 2:10 and Col 1:16).

The series of different names to describe the powers and the authorities assumedly residing in those heavenly places are not to be taken as referring to actual angelic beings, as was mistakenly done in classical theology.[11] Rather it is intended to be a literary

---

[11] Theology's fascination with preexistence and mysticism ended with the ridiculous conception of the nine levels of angelic powers: Seraphim, Cherubim, Thrones, Dominions, Virtues, Powers, Principalities, Archangels, Angels. See already in the sixth

inclusiveness of all *kinds* of governing powers, whether political (Rome) or religious (Jerusalem), that assumed a "divine" or "heavenly" authority, if not origin.[12] It is not a detailed enumeration of actual "standings" in the manner of terms the like of emperor, high priest, governor, or centurion. This is clear from the varied lengths of the series:

whether thrones or dominions or principalities or authorities. (Col 1:16)

and you have come to fulness of life in him, who is the head of all rule and authority. (Col 2:10)

Then comes the end, when he delivers the kingdom to God the Father after destroying every rule and every authority and power. (1 Cor 15:24)

who has gone into heaven and is at the right hand of God, with angels, authorities, and powers subject to him. (1 Pet 3:22)

That the series is intended to be a literary device aiming at inclusiveness is apparent in Ephesians:

far above all rule and authority and power and dominion, and above every name that is named, not only in this age but also in that which is to come. (1:21)

What lends further support to this assertion is the phraseology revolving around the term "name" in Philippians:

Therefore God has highly exalted him and bestowed on him the name which is above every name, that at the name of Jesus every knee should bow, in heaven and on earth and under the earth. (2:9-10)

century Pseudo-Dionysius the Areopagite's *De Coelesti Hierarchia* (On the Celestial Hierarchy) and later Thomas Aquinas' *Summa Theologica.*

[12] The Roman emperor was deified in his lifetime and the Jewish leaders in Jerusalem assumed to be the spokesmen of the scriptural God.

Since Philippians is canonically heard after Ephesians, the hearer cannot help but link the two passages and understand that "and every name that is named" after "rule and authority and power and dominion" (Eph 1:21) is simply intended to mean "any such kind of authority."

Again a common presupposition in classical theology is that, given the "cosmic" phraseology of vv.20-21 and its misrepresentation along Platonic lines, the church referred to in v.22 (and also later in 3:21) is readily assumed to be first and foremost an eternal and cosmic entity or reality that is secondarily "reflected" in the "local" churches. Such view is readily contradicted through the representation of the church as the body of Christ and, more so, as a parenthetical insertion before the resumption of the "cosmic" terminology. Add to this that the apparently "additional" phrase regarding the body is nonetheless intentional since it was already on the author's mind in the immediately preceding phrase "and gave him *to be* the[13] head over all *things* to the church" (Eph 1:22 KJV).[14] In other words, God has gifted Christ to the church, which is the recipient of the gift,[15] and he has placed Christ in the function, the position, of its head. It is evident that the choice of "head" was made in view of the following metaphor of the "body" (v.23). Unless one's mind has been formatted by later theological jargon, unbiased hearers cannot miss the link to what they heard earlier in 1 Corinthians 12 where the metaphor of the church as body is developed in a detailed and repetitive manner.[16] The term "body" occurs no less than seventeen times culminating with the statement "Now you are the body of Christ" (1 Cor 12:27), which is precisely what is heard at the conclusion of Ephesians 1. The link with 1

---

[13] Not in the original. More accurately "gave (placed, posited) him (as) head."

[14] I chose KJV because its rendering of the original is more accurate than the very poor translation of RSV.

[15] In Greek *tē ekklēsia* is in the dative, that is to say, functions as an indirect complement to the verb *edōken.*

[16] The reference to Christ as "head" occurred earlier in 1 Cor 11:13.

Corinthians is unmissable given that later in Ephesians we hear the statements "the Gentiles are fellow heirs, members of the same body" (3:6) and "because we are members of his body" (5:30), and given also that the noun "member" is a staple of 1 Corinthians 11 (vv.12 [twice], 14, 25, 26 [twice], 27). What is ultimately the most compelling feature is that the "you" of 1 Corinthians 12:27 are none other than the recipients of the letter who are addressed as "the church of God *which is at Corinth*" (1:2), a form of address iterated in 2 Corinthians (1:1b). This precludes the notion, fabricated by theology devised by Greco-Romans, of a "cosmic" church and a "cosmic" body of Christ. How can a body with members such as foot or hand (1 Cor 12:14), ear or eye (v.15) be cosmic? Such theology wants us to believe that members of a Roman household sitting around a dinner table to partake of a common meal (11:20-22), eating bread and drinking a cup of wine (v.28), would have understood Paul's words à la such theology. Two points are in order here. On the one hand, the phrase "eat of the *bread* and drink of the *cup*" (v.28) occurs *after* the so-called "words of institution" of classical theology. On the other hand, the "body" which is supposed to be discerned is the church community: "For any one who eats and drinks without discerning the body eats and drinks judgment upon himself." (v. 29)[17]

The conclusion imposes itself. The "church" in Pauline lingo is always and exclusively the *kat' oikon ekklēsia* that is greeted (Rom 16:5; Col 4:15) or sends greetings (Rom 16:19) or is addressed (Philem 1). Unfortunately, this phrase is always translated and perceived as meaning "house church" in the sense of "a church that gathers in a house." One begins with an assumed mental perception of what a church is, i.e., a kind of mystical cosmic church that is gathered in a family house instead of in a synagogue or in a temple or any given building (Acts 16:15; 17:5; 18:7). The problem with this understanding is that one can justify the later construction of self-standing large buildings—ending up with

---

[17] See on both counts my comments in *C-1Cor* 202-15.

colossal monuments—to host a "church" that no longer fits size wise in a family house. In such case, the preposition *kata*[18] before *oikon* is taken as meaning simply "in"—reflecting location—as in RSV and KJV: "church in their house" (Rom 16:5, 19), "church in her[19] house" (Col 4:15), "church in your house" (Philem 1).[20] However, *kata* does not reflect the meaning of "in" since the author could have readily used the expression *en oikō* "in (the) house." The preposition *kata* is followed by either the genitive (possessive) case with the connotation of "down from" or "against," or by the accusative (noun complement) case with the connotation of "according to"—as in *kata Markon* (according to Mark; à la Mark)—or "throughout a period of time." Thus the precise rendering of *kat' oikon ekklēsia* is "household church" rather than "house church." This is linguistically supported in that both the Hebrew *bet* (house) and the Greek *oikos* or *oikia* have the double connotation of house and household, as evidenced in all translations. Furthermore, the same is supported by the fact that "believers" are often referred to with nouns and adjectives— *oikeios*,[21] *oiketēs*,[22] *oikiakos*[23]—whose literal meaning is "house-ly/ies," "domestic/s" —from the Latin *domus* (house; household)—which has been captured by the Vulgate translators. Compare the Latin with the Greek in the following two instances:

---

[18] Contracted into *kat'* before a vowel.

[19] "his" in KJV where Nymphas is taken as a man's, and not a woman's, name.

[20] The same is found in French and Arabic.

[21] Gal 6:10; 1 Tim 5:8. Important for our discussion is that, although *kat' oikon ekklēsia* is not found in Ephesians, yet one hears of *oikeioi* in conjunction with no less than five nouns built around the root *oik—*: "So then you are no longer strangers and sojourners (*paroikoi*), but you are fellow citizens with the saints and *members of the household* (*oikeioi*; Latin *domestici*) of God, built (*epoikodomēthentes*) upon the foundation of the apostles and prophets, Christ Jesus himself being the cornerstone, in whom the whole structure (*oikodomē*; building) is joined together and grows into a holy temple in the Lord; in whom you also are built into (*synoikodomeisthe*) it for a dwelling place (*katoikētērion*) of God in the Spirit." (Eph 2:19-22)

[22] Lk 16:13; Acts 10:7; Rom 14:4; 1 Pet 2:18.

[23] Mt 10:25, 36.

greet also the church in their house (Greek *kat' oikon ekklēsia*; Latin *domesticam ecclesiam* [domestic/housely church]). Greet my beloved Epaenetus, who was the first convert in Asia for Christ. (Rom 16:5)

The churches of Asia send greetings. Aquila and Prisca, together with the church in their house (Greek *kat' oikon ekklēsia*; Latin *domesticam ecclesiam* [domestic/housely church]), send you hearty greetings in the Lord. (1 Cor 16:19)

As always, Paul's world of reference is the Roman empire, and not a theoretical ontological world of Jew versus Gentile. That is why, after having established the oneness of the Jew and the Gentile in the same household church, he goes back to underscoring that this new reality is not under the authority of Caesar, but is under that of God's crucified messiah, who is both emperor and *paterfamilias*. Indeed, Christ became the head of all rule (*arkhēs*) and authority (*exousias*) (Col 2:10) since God disarmed all principalities (*arkhas*; ruling powers) and powers (*exousias*; authorities) and triumphed over them publicly in Christ (v.15). "Disarmed" is the translation of the Greek *apekdysamenos* (took off their clothing), which is the same verb that is used earlier in v.11 to speak of "putting off the body of flesh." The hearer cannot miss this link which confirms Paul's intent to say that Christ has become functionally for the believers the true emperor and *paterfamilias*, that is to say, the head of both the empire and every believing household in it. Whereas the emperor was apotheosed (deified) by senatorial decree, Jesus Christ acceded to that honor by the decree of God himself (Phil 2:9-10). So, all in all, Paul is not establishing a universal or cosmological "church" to supplant the Roman empire. Rather he is planting seeds of the Kingdom in as many households as possible in order to lead the *empire* (unquestioned authority), constructed around the apotheosis of a lineage of mere humans, away from its hubris and back to the original Roman polity that is tribal in essence, built around "households" (*bet 'ab*) each ruled by an elder who is the *paterfamilias*. Nevertheless, the totality of the households is "joined together as one building" (Eph 2:20) under the tutelage and absolute authority of the scriptural God (vv.18 and 22) who is the one and sole Father of all: "For this reason I bow my knees before the Father, from whom every family (*patria*; fatherhood; a community around a father figure [paterfamilias])[24] in heaven and on earth is named." (Eph 3:14-15) Noticeable is the multiplicity of such "units," which is reflected in the phrase "every (*pasa*) family (*patria*)."[25] The "how" of this Pauline endeavor is the subject matter of Ephesians 2.

---

[24] The French *patrie* refers to the nation.
[25] See on this matter in more detail the chapter "Common Table Fellowship" in my *The Rise of Scripture*, 335-41.

Chapter 2

Vv. 1-22 ¹Καὶ ὑμᾶς ὄντας νεκροὺς τοῖς παραπτώμασιν καὶ ταῖς ἁμαρτίαις ὑμῶν ²ἐν αἷς ποτε περιεπατήσατε κατὰ τὸν αἰῶνα τοῦ κόσμου τούτου κατὰ τὸν ἄρχοντα τῆς ἐξουσίας τοῦ ἀέρος τοῦ πνεύματος τοῦ νῦν ἐνεργοῦντος ἐν τοῖς υἱοῖς τῆς ἀπειθείας· ³ἐν οἷς καὶ ἡμεῖς πάντες ἀνεστράφημέν ποτε ἐν ταῖς ἐπιθυμίαις τῆς σαρκὸς ἡμῶν ποιοῦντες τὰ θελήματα τῆς σαρκὸς καὶ τῶν διανοιῶν καὶ ἤμεθα τέκνα φύσει ὀργῆς ὡς καὶ οἱ λοιποί· ⁴ὁ δὲ θεὸς πλούσιος ὢν ἐν ἐλέει διὰ τὴν πολλὴν ἀγάπην αὐτοῦ ἣν ἠγάπησεν ἡμᾶς ⁵καὶ ὄντας ἡμᾶς νεκροὺς τοῖς παραπτώμασιν συνεζωοποίησεν τῷ Χριστῷ χάριτί ἐστε σεσῳσμένοῖ ⁶καὶ συνήγειρεν καὶ συνεκάθισεν ἐν τοῖς ἐπουρανίοις ἐν Χριστῷ Ἰησοῦ ⁷ἵνα ἐνδείξηται ἐν τοῖς αἰῶσιν τοῖς ἐπερχομένοις τὸ ὑπερβάλλον πλοῦτος τῆς χάριτος αὐτοῦ ἐν χρηστότητι ἐφ᾽ ἡμᾶς ἐν Χριστῷ Ἰησοῦ ⁸Τῇ γὰρ χάριτί ἐστε σεσῳσμένοι διὰ πίστεως· καὶ τοῦτο οὐκ ἐξ ὑμῶν· θεοῦ τὸ δῶρον· ⁹οὐκ ἐξ ἔργων· ἵνα μή τις καυχήσηταῖ ¹⁰αὐτοῦ γάρ ἐσμεν ποίημά κτισθέντες ἐν Χριστῷ Ἰησοῦ ἐπὶ ἔργοις ἀγαθοῖς οἷς προητοίμασεν ὁ θεὸς ἵνα ἐν αὐτοῖς περιπατήσωμεν ¹¹Διὸ μνημονεύετε ὅτι ποτὲ ὑμεῖς τὰ ἔθνη ἐν σαρκί οἱ λεγόμενοι ἀκροβυστία ὑπὸ τῆς λεγομένης περιτομῆς ἐν σαρκὶ χειροποιήτου ¹²ὅτι ἦτε τῷ καιρῷ ἐκείνῳ χωρὶς Χριστοῦ ἀπηλλοτριωμένοι τῆς πολιτείας τοῦ Ἰσραὴλ καὶ ξένοι τῶν διαθηκῶν τῆς ἐπαγγελίας ἐλπίδα μὴ ἔχοντες καὶ ἄθεοι ἐν τῷ κόσμῳ· ¹³νυνὶ δὲ ἐν Χριστῷ Ἰησοῦ ὑμεῖς οἵ ποτε ὄντες μακρὰν ἐγενήθητε ἐγγὺς ἐν τῷ αἵματι τοῦ Χριστοῦ ¹⁴Αὐτὸς γάρ ἐστιν ἡ εἰρήνη ἡμῶν ὁ ποιήσας τὰ ἀμφότερα ἓν καὶ τὸ μεσότοιχον τοῦ φραγμοῦ λύσας τὴν ἔχθραν ἐν τῇ σαρκὶ αὐτοῦ¹⁵τὸν νόμον τῶν ἐντολῶν ἐν δόγμασιν καταργήσας ἵνα τοὺς δύο κτίσῃ ἐν αὐτῷ εἰς ἕνα καινὸν ἄνθρωπον ποιῶν εἰρήνην ¹⁶καὶ ἀποκαταλλάξῃ τοὺς ἀμφοτέρους ἐν ἑνὶ σώματι τῷ θεῷ διὰ τοῦ σταυροῦ ἀποκτείνας τὴν ἔχθραν ἐν αὐτῷ ¹⁷καὶ ἐλθὼν εὐηγγελίσατο εἰρήνην ὑμῖν τοῖς μακρὰν καὶ εἰρήνην τοῖς ἐγγύς· ¹⁸ὅτι δι᾽ αὐτοῦ ἔχομεν τὴν προσαγωγὴν οἱ ἀμφότεροι ἐν ἑνὶ πνεύματι πρὸς τὸν πατέρα· ¹⁹Ἄρα οὖν οὐκέτι ἐστὲ ξένοι καὶ πάροικοι ἀλλὰ ἐστὲ συμπολῖται τῶν ἁγίων καὶ οἰκεῖοι τοῦ θεοῦ ²⁰ἐποικοδομηθέντες ἐπὶ τῷ θεμελίῳ τῶν ἀποστόλων καὶ προφητῶν ὄντος ἀκρογωνιαίου αὐτοῦ Χριστοῦ Ἰησοῦ ²¹ἐν ᾧ πᾶσα οἰκοδομὴ συναρμολογουμένη αὔξει εἰς ναὸν ἅγιον ἐν κυρίῳ ²²ἐν ᾧ καὶ ὑμεῖς συνοικοδομεῖσθε εἰς κατοικητήριον τοῦ θεοῦ ἐν πνεύματι

¹And you he made alive, when you were dead through the trespasses and sins ²in which you once walked, following the course of this world, following the prince of the power of the air, the spirit that is now at work in the sons of disobedience. ³Among these we all once lived in the passions of our flesh, following the desires of body and mind, and so we were by nature children of wrath, like the rest of mankind. ⁴But God, who is rich in mercy, out of the great love with which he loved us, ⁵even when we were dead through our trespasses, made us alive together with Christ (by grace you have been saved), ⁶and raised us up with him, and made us sit with him in the heavenly places in Christ Jesus, ⁷that in the coming ages he might show the immeasurable riches of his grace in kindness toward us in Christ Jesus. ⁸For by grace you have been saved through faith; and this is not your own doing, it is the gift of God—⁹not because of works, lest any man should boast. ¹⁰For we are his workmanship, created in Christ Jesus for good works, which God prepared beforehand, that we should walk in them. ¹¹Therefore remember that at one time you Gentiles in the flesh, called the uncircumcision by what is called the circumcision, which is made in the flesh by hands—¹²remember that you were at that time separated from Christ, alienated from the commonwealth of Israel, and strangers to the covenants of promise, having no hope and without God in the world. ¹³But now in Christ Jesus you who once were far off have been brought near in the blood of Christ. ¹⁴For he is our peace, who has made us both one, and has broken down the dividing wall of hostility, ¹⁵by abolishing in his flesh the law of commandments and ordinances, that he might create in himself one new man in place of the two, so making peace, ¹⁶and might reconcile us both to God in one body through the cross,

thereby bringing the hostility to an end. [17]And he came and preached peace to you who were far off and peace to those who were near; [18]for through him we both have access in one Spirit to the Father. [19]So then you are no longer strangers and sojourners, but you are fellow citizens with the saints and members of the household of God, [20]built upon the foundation of the apostles and prophets, Christ Jesus himself being the cornerstone, [21]in whom the whole structure is joined together and grows into a holy temple in the Lord; [22]in whom you also are built into it for a dwelling place of God in the Spirit.

In chapter 1 Paul made it clear that the only way for the Gentiles to be party to the expectation of the scriptural Israel is for them to be aligned with that Israel in the story of the Old Testament. It is only thus that Gentiles will be on par with Israel in God's heavenly city (Is 66): "Now these things happened to them as a warning, but they were written down for our instruction, upon whom the end of the ages has come." (1 Cor 10:11) Through his preaching Paul has established that his Gentiles have been put in line with the Jews under the umbrella of the Old Testament teaching.[1] He covered this in Galatians 3:1-14 using express quotations not only from the Torah (Genesis in vv.6 and 8; Leviticus in v.12; Deuteronomy in vv.10 and 13), but also from the Prophets (namely, Habakuk, v.11), and ending with the blessing through the promise to both Jews and Gentiles: "that in Christ Jesus the blessing of Abraham might come upon the Gentiles, that we might receive the promise of the Spirit through faith." (v.14).[2]

In Ephesians 2 Paul continues to follow closely the blue print of Galatians, making it clear that the Gentiles are put in line with scriptural Israel not through mental knowledge of the Old Testament and its contents, as was promoted by Alexandrian theology, but rather through the realization that both Jews and Gentiles have sinned through disobedience to the dictates of God's law and, consequently, have earned divine wrath (Eph 2:1-

---

[1] He did this by using in abundance the preposition *pro* (before, ahead, beforehand).

[2] See my extensive discussion of that entire passage in *Gal* 134-7.

4). It is solely due to God's love that his wrath did not fully prevail (v.5). This was introduced at the beginning of the letter: "He destined us in love to be his sons through Jesus Christ, according to the purpose of his will." (1:5) Just as in 1:5, God's love was poured through the medium of Jesus Christ (2:5-7) exclusively, as is evident in the repeated "by grace you have been saved" at the beginning and at the end of the statement concerning Christ (vv.5 and 8a). Paul did not want to leave any shred of a doubt regarding this matter, so he wraps up this passage with the emphatically unequivocal: "and this is not your own doing, it is the gift of God—not because of works, lest any man should boast." (vv.8b-9). This is not to be perceived as a license for the Gentiles to revel in having been recipients of God's gift and bask in a mystical aura as though they are *already* saved or, worse, *already* in the kingdom, which has not come yet.[3] The reason therefor, as Paul wrote in Galatians 5:13-16 and emphasized again in Ephesians, is that God's free—without charge (fee)—gift still comes with his charge (command) to do his will: "For we are his workmanship, created in Christ Jesus for good works, which God prepared beforehand, *that we should walk in them.*" (Eph 2:10). The astuteness lies in the differentiation between God's work and ours. In the original Greek "workmanship" is *poiēma* while works is *ergois.* Technically *poiēma* is product or result of one's doing, which is from the verb *poi(e)ō* that is used in Genesis 1 (LXX) describing God's action of making (producing) the heavens, the earth, and the waters and their denizens, without any consultation. In the same way, our salvation is exclusively and one-sidedly the result of God's doing. On the other hand, the good "works" required of us were *preordained* (***proētoimasen***) by him. Put otherwise, dealing with God's gift does not consist in simply receiving or accepting it; dealing with it means "handling" it. Moreover, the handling itself cannot be according to our will or whim, but must be according

---

[3] As usual and against what Paul had cautioned in Galatians 1:6-9, classical theology in all its forms ends up by being a "tradition of men" that not only misses the mark but squarely and thoroughly contradicts the gospel teaching.

to God's will and instructions.[4] However, one should not quickly conclude from Ephesians 2:10 that the differentiation between "doing" and "works" is set in stone, and then make unwarranted theological generalizations. Scripture is plain literature where the meaning and function of words depends on the immediate context. A case in point can be found in Philippians where, in order to forego self-gratification on our part, Paul goes even further than he does in Ephesians by stating that the same God who foreordains the works (*ergois*) we are bound to do, is actually in absolute control of our activity itself: "Therefore, my beloved, as you have always obeyed, so now, not only as in my presence but much more in my absence, work out (*katergazesthe*) your own salvation with fear and trembling; for God is at work (*energōn*) in you, both to will and to work (*energein*) for his good pleasure." (Phil 2:12-13)[5] Here the same root *erg*— is used to depict the actions of both God and us. So the play is on a different level: although we have to fulfill, that is, to bring to full completion, the work needed to implement our salvation, it is ultimately God who energizes (pours the energy into) us to will that action and to put it to work. Thus, theological overarching conclusions should be banned because they ultimately express our presuppositions or, worse, predilections. Every theological endeavor is ultimately a *summa theologica*, an artificial summation of our own conclusions. To put it metaphorically, whereas theology functions as a treatise of physiology, the scriptural text remains the actual physiological "body" that is always there to force us into rewriting and updating our physiology manuals.

If the ultimate salvation will not take place save at the judgment of whether our "works" will have been good according to God's requirements,[6] then Ephesians 2:5b-6 (made us alive together with Christ [by grace you have been saved], and raised us up with him,

---

[4] This brings to mind the warning on purchased appliances or furniture or games that require assembly or even mere usage: "Read the instructions *before* (Greek *pro*) handling."

[5] See my comments in *C-Phil* 134-5.

[6] And I am sure that he who began a good work in you will bring it to completion at the day of Jesus Christ. (Phil 1:6)

and made us sit with him in the heavenly places in Christ Jesus) cannot possibly be interpreted as though we are *already* "in heavens whence we await a Savior, the Lord Jesus Christ, who *will change* (future tense *metaskhēmatisei*) our lowly body to be like his glorious body, by the power which enables him even to subject all things to himself." (Phil 3:20-21) Such an interpretation has led to endless discussions about "realized eschatology" or at least "inaugurated eschatology." If such were the case, then the teaching in Ephesians 2 would contradict that in Romans 6-8.

It is due to the misunderstanding of the Greek "aorist" (*aoristos*) modal tense, that verses 5b-6 in Ephesians 2 have often been erroneously taken to mean that the addressees were already experiencing the kingdom here and now. Recent language studies have shown that verbal forms are to be approached modally, from the perspective of the action, rather than temporally, from the perspective of time divided into past, present, and future. Take, for instance, the English, "I shall have eaten" or even simply "having eaten." Is the action of eating already consummated or not? The "have eaten" militates for the former, whereas the "shall have eaten" for the latter. The dilemma is solved only when one approaches the matter not temporally, but views the action of eating in conjunction with another action: "After I shall have eaten (having eaten), I shall go to the movies." The eating is before the going, yet it is still in the future. Thus functions the "aorist," which is a transliteration of *aoristos* meaning "without horizon, non-delineated, undefined." It is essentially a modal verbal form expressing the completeness of the action disregarding the time element. Consequently, it expresses the assuredness of the action referred to, rather than the time it takes place. This is precisely what Ephesians 2:5b-6 is trying to convey: assuredness that is provided to the Ephesians in order that they maintain their resolve. This is confirmed in verse 10 where Paul asks them to "walk in the good works God pre-ordained for them." To further illustrate my point, let me quote the striking instance of Romans 8:24-25: "For in this hope *we were saved* (*esōthēmen* [aorist]). Now hope that is seen is not hope. For who hopes for what he sees? But if we hope for what we do not see, we wait for (*apekdekhometha*) it with patience."[7] The salvation Paul is speaking of in these verses lies ahead, yet it is expressed in the aorist tense, which reflects the assuredness of our salvation *should we wait with patience*. This understanding is supported in what Paul wrote a few verses earlier: "For you did not receive the spirit of slavery to fall back into fear, but you have received the spirit of sonship. When we cry 'Abba! Father!' it is the Spirit himself bearing witness with our spirit that we are children of God, and if children, then heirs, heirs of God and fellow heirs with Christ, *provided we suffer with him in order that we may also be glorified with him*."(vv.15-17)

If the Gentiles are to abide by God's pre-ordained will for them, then the question that arises is, "How would they become aware of that will?" The only answer is unequivocally given time and again in the Pauline corpus: by making them privy to hearing the dictates of the Law, as was made clear as early on as Joshua 8:33-35. That is why Paul repeatedly underscored the oneness of Gentiles and Jews, the "being at one," that is, one entity under the scriptural God's overarching "tent of the meeting." This "one" *oikos* "house(hold)" is patterned here after the Roman house(hold) where individuals of "all nations" live as one community.[8] This is precisely what Paul states in the second part of Ephesians 2:11-22, using the same approach found in the companion letter to the

---

[7] See also Galatians 5:4-5 where our being declared righteous, although based on faith, is still a matter of hope and thus to be awaited: "You are severed from Christ, you who would be justified by the law; you have fallen away from grace. For through the Spirit, by faith, we wait for (*apekdekhometha*) the hope of righteousness." It is worth noting here that the third instance of *apekdekhometha* in the Pauline corpus occurs in conjunction with the "yet to come" Savior: "But our commonwealth is in heaven, and from it we await (*apekdekhometha*) a Savior, the Lord Jesus Christ, who *will change* (future tense) our lowly body to be like his glorious body, by the power which enables him even to subject all things to himself." (Phil 3:20-21) See also in this regard "so that you are not lacking in any spiritual gift, as you wait (*apekdekhomenous*) for the *revealing* (*apokalypsin*) of our Lord Jesus Christ" (1 Cor 1:7).

[8] See my comments on the speaking in different tongues (1 Cor 14) in *C-1Cor* 245-9.

Colossians,[9] as is evident when comparing the vocabulary of the two letters, in spite of the fact that Colossians does not use the term "building":

> Therefore remember that at one time you Gentiles in the flesh, called the uncircumcision by what is called the circumcision, which is made in the flesh by hands—remember that you were at that time separated from Christ, alienated from the commonwealth (*politeias*) of Israel, and strangers to the covenants of promise, having no hope and without God in the world. But now in Christ Jesus you who once were far off have been brought near in the blood of Christ. For he is our peace, who has made us both one, and has broken down the dividing wall of hostility, by abolishing in his flesh the law of commandments and ordinances, that he might create in himself one new man in place of the two, so making peace, and might reconcile us both to God in one body through the cross, thereby bringing the hostility to an end. And he came and preached peace to you who were far off and peace to those who were near; for through him we both have access in one Spirit to the Father. So then you are no longer strangers and sojourners (*paroikoi*), but you are fellow citizens (*sympolitai*) with the saints and members of the household (*oikeioi*) of God, built upon (*epikodomēthentes*) the foundation of the apostles and prophets, Christ Jesus himself being the cornerstone, in whom the whole structure (*oikodomē*) is joined together and grows into a holy temple in the Lord; in whom you also are built into it (*synoikodomeisthe*) for a dwelling place (*katoikētērion*) of God in the Spirit. (Eph 2:1-22)

For in him all the fulness of God was pleased to dwell (*katoikēsai*), and through him to reconcile to himself all things, whether on earth or in heaven, making peace by the blood of his cross. And you, who once were estranged and hostile in mind, doing evil deeds, he has now reconciled in his body of flesh by his death, in order to present you holy and blameless and irreproachable before him, provided that you continue in the faith, stable and steadfast, not shifting from

---

[9] My readers are reminded that both Ephesus and Colossae lie in the Roman province Asia.

the hope of the gospel which you heard, which has been preached to every creature under heaven, and of which I, Paul, became a minister.[10] Now I rejoice in my sufferings for your sake, and in my flesh I complete what is lacking in Christ's afflictions for the sake of his body, that is, the church, of which I became a minister according to the divine office (*oikonomian*; plan) which was given to me for you, to make the word of God fully known, the mystery hidden for ages and generations but now made manifest to his saints. (Col 1:19-26)

As therefore you received Christ Jesus the Lord, so live in him, rooted and built up (*epoikodomoumenoi*) in him and established in the faith, just as you were taught, abounding in thanksgiving. See to it that no one makes a prey of you by philosophy and empty deceit, according to human tradition, according to the elemental spirits of the universe, and not according to Christ. For in him the whole fulness of deity dwells (*katoikei*) bodily. (2:6-9)

Let the word of Christ dwell in (*enoikeitō*) you richly, teach and admonish one another in all wisdom, and sing psalms and hymns and spiritual songs with thankfulness in your hearts to God. (3:16)

The least one can say about the compared texts is that they are copycats of one another except for a striking feature in Ephesians that is nowhere to be found in the entire letter to the Colossians, which is the root *poli(t)*— that relates to "city" (*politeias* in Eph 2:12 and *sympolitai* in v.19). The oddity is enhanced by the fact that this root is encountered in Philippians, the third Captivity Epistle:

Only let your manner of life (*politevesthe*; behave as a citizen of a polity would) be worthy of the gospel of Christ, so that whether I come and see you or am absent, I may hear of you that you stand firm in one spirit, with one mind striving side by side for the faith of the gospel, (Phil 1:27)

---

[10] Compare with Eph 3:7: "Of this gospel I was made a minister according to the gift of God's grace which was given me by the working of his power."

So then you are no longer strangers and sojourners, but you are fellow citizens (*sympolitai*) with the saints and members of the household of God. (2:19)

But our commonwealth (*politevma*) is in heaven, and from it we await a Savior, the Lord Jesus Christ. (3:20)

This confirms that the author of Ephesians is viewing the "church" where both Gentiles and Jews stand—or more accurately sit (at the fellowship table where Paul ministers to them both as a *diakonos* would)—on an equal footing under the aegis of God, and not under that of the Roman emperor. That it is the Roman household, and not empire, that defines the ethos of Paul's churches is substantiated in a singular feature of Ephesians where the *sympolitai* (fellow citizens) of the "saints"—that is, the Pauline believers—are presented as *oikeioi* (members of the household) of God (Eph 2:19). We have the seal that the church is cast as "the household of God" in 1 Timothy:

I hope to come to you soon, but I am writing these instructions to you so that, if I am delayed, you may know how one ought to behave in the household of God (*oikō Theou*), which is the church of the living God (*hetis estin ekklēsia Theou zōntos*), the pillar and bulwark of the truth. (3:14-15)

Chapter 3

Vv. 1-21 ¹Τούτου χάριν ἐγὼ Παῦλος ὁ δέσμιος τοῦ Χριστοῦ Ἰησοῦ ὑπὲρ ὑμῶν τῶν ἐθνῶν ²εἴ γε ἠκούσατε τὴν οἰκονομίαν τῆς χάριτος τοῦ θεοῦ τῆς δοθείσης μοι εἰς ὑμᾶς ³ὅτΐ κατὰ ἀποκάλυψιν ἐγνωρίσθη μοι τὸ μυστήριόν καθὼς προέγραψα ἐν ὀλίγῳ ⁴πρὸς ὃ δύνασθε ἀναγινώσκοντες νοῆσαι τὴν σύνεσίν μου ἐν τῷ μυστηρίῳ τοῦ Χριστοῦ ⁵ὃ ἑτέραις γενεαῖς οὐκ ἐγνωρίσθη τοῖς υἱοῖς τῶν ἀνθρώπων ὡς νῦν ἀπεκαλύφθη τοῖς ἁγίοις ἀποστόλοις αὐτοῦ καὶ προφήταις ἐν πνεύματί ⁶εἶναι τὰ ἔθνη συγκληρονόμα καὶ σύσσωμα καὶ συμμέτοχα τῆς ἐπαγγελίας ἐν Χριστῷ Ἰησοῦ διὰ τοῦ εὐαγγελίού ⁷οὗ ἐγενήθην διάκονος κατὰ τὴν δωρεὰν τῆς χάριτος τοῦ θεοῦ τῆς δοθείσης μοι κατὰ τὴν ἐνέργειαν τῆς δυνάμεως αὐτοῦ ⁸Ἐμοὶ τῷ ἐλαχιστοτέρῳ πάντων ἁγίων ἐδόθη ἡ χάρις αὕτή τοῖς ἔθνεσιν εὐαγγελίσασθαι τὸ ἀνεξιχνίαστον πλοῦτος τοῦ Χριστοῦ ⁹καὶ φωτίσαι πάνταϛ τίς ἡ οἰκονομία τοῦ μυστηρίου τοῦ ἀποκεκρυμμένου ἀπὸ τῶν αἰώνων ἐν τῷ θεῷ τῷ τὰ πάντα κτίσαντί ¹⁰ἵνα γνωρισθῇ νῦν ταῖς ἀρχαῖς καὶ ταῖς ἐξουσίαις ἐν τοῖς ἐπουρανίοις διὰ τῆς ἐκκλησίας ἡ πολυποίκιλος σοφία τοῦ θεοῦ ¹¹κατὰ πρόθεσιν τῶν αἰώνων ἣν ἐποίησεν ἐν τῷ Χριστῷ Ἰησοῦ τῷ κυρίῳ ἡμῶν ¹²ἐν ᾧ ἔχομεν τὴν παρρησίαν καὶ προσαγωγὴν ἐν πεποιθήσει διὰ τῆς πίστεως αὐτοῦ ¹³διὸ αἰτοῦμαι μὴ ἐγκακεῖν ἐν ταῖς θλίψεσίν μου ὑπὲρ ὑμῶν ἥτις ἐστὶν δόξα ὑμῶν ¹⁴Τούτου χάριν κάμπτω τὰ γόνατά μου πρὸς τὸν πατέρά ¹⁵ἐξ οὗ πᾶσα πατριὰ ἐν οὐρανοῖς καὶ ἐπὶ γῆς ὀνομάζεταί ¹⁶ἵνα δῷ ὑμῖν κατὰ τὸ πλοῦτος τῆς δόξης αὐτοῦ δυνάμει κραταιωθῆναι διὰ τοῦ πνεύματος αὐτοῦ εἰς τὸν ἔσω ἄνθρωπόν ¹⁷κατοικῆσαι τὸν Χριστὸν διὰ τῆς πίστεως ἐν ταῖς καρδίαις ὑμῶν ἐν ἀγάπῃ ἐρριζωμένοι καὶ τεθεμελιωμένοί ¹⁸ἵνα ἐξισχύσητε καταλαβέσθαι σὺν πᾶσιν τοῖς ἁγίοις τί τὸ πλάτος καὶ μῆκος καὶ ὕψος καὶ βάθος ¹⁹γνῶναί τε τὴν ὑπερβάλλουσαν τῆς γνώσεως ἀγάπην τοῦ Χριστοῦ ἵνα πληρωθῆτε εἰς πᾶν

69

τὸ πλήρωμα τοῦ θεοῦ ²⁰Τῷ δὲ δυναμένῳ ὑπὲρ πάντα ποιῆσαι ὑπερεκπερισσοῦ ὧν αἰτούμεθα ἢ νοοῦμεν κατὰ τὴν δύναμιν τὴν ἐνεργουμένην ἐν ἡμῖν ²¹αὐτῷ ἡ δόξα ἐν τῇ ἐκκλησίᾳ καὶ ἐν Χριστῷ Ἰησοῦ εἰς πάσας τὰς γενεὰς τοῦ αἰῶνος τῶν αἰώνων· ἀμήν

¹For this reason I, Paul, a prisoner for Christ Jesus on behalf of you Gentiles—²assuming that you have heard of the stewardship of God's grace that was given to me for you, ³how the mystery was made known to me by revelation, as I have written briefly. ⁴When you read this you can perceive my insight into the mystery of Christ, ⁵which was not made known to the sons of men in other generations as it has now been revealed to his holy apostles and prophets by the Spirit; ⁶that is, how the Gentiles are fellow heirs, members of the same body, and partakers of the promise in Christ Jesus through the gospel. ⁷Of this gospel I was made a minister according to the gift of God's grace which was given me by the working of his power. ⁸To me, though I am the very least of all the saints, this grace was given, to preach to the Gentiles the unsearchable riches of Christ, ⁹and to make all men see what is the plan of the mystery hidden for ages in God who created all things; ¹⁰that through the church the manifold wisdom of God might now be made known to the principalities and powers in the heavenly places. ¹¹This was according to the eternal purpose which he has realized in Christ Jesus our Lord, ¹²in whom we have boldness and confidence of access through our faith in him. ¹³So I ask you not to lose heart over what I am suffering for you, which is your glory. ¹⁴For this reason I bow my knees before the Father, ¹⁵from whom every family in heaven and on earth is named, ¹⁶that according to the riches of his glory he may grant you to be strengthened with might through his Spirit in the inner man, ¹⁷and that Christ may dwell in your hearts through faith; that you, being rooted and grounded in love, ¹⁸may have power to comprehend with all the saints what is the breadth and length and height and depth, ¹⁹and to know the love of Christ which surpasses knowledge, that you may be filled with all the fulness of God. ²⁰Now to him who by the power at work within us is able to do far more abundantly than all that we ask or think, ²¹to him be glory in the church and in Christ Jesus to all generations, for ever and ever. Amen.

That Paul presents himself as the apostle to the Gentiles and the agent who brought the teaching of the "holy scriptures" *as gospel* (Rom 1:1-2) to them is a staple of all his letters. So Ephesians 3 is not at all unexpected in view of the "plan" of God that was introduced in chapters 1 and 2, according to which the Gentiles would eventually join the "polity" of the scriptural Israel.

A caveat is in order here. Very often the term "mystery" (3:3, 4, 9) has been misconstrued to mean something that remains enigmatic and only those who are somehow illumined can comprehend it. In turn, this illumination is viewed as a "spiritual" event to which one accedes under the guidance of a "spiritual" mentor. Such would be a *disciplina arcana* that is revealed only to the chosen few, similar to the priestly *torah* (hidden teaching) which was criticized by God through his *debarim* (open words) that filled his prophets' mouths.[1] Paul comments on this matter at the end of Romans:

> Now to him who is able to strengthen you according to my gospel and the preaching of Jesus Christ, according to the revelation of the mystery which was kept secret for long ages but is now made manifest *(phanerōthentos)* and through the prophetic writings is made known *(gnōristhentos)* to all the nations *(eis panta ta ethnē)*, according to the command of the eternal God, to bring about the obedience of faith—to the only wise God be glory for evermore through Jesus Christ! Amen. (16:25-26)

The parallelism with Ephesians 3:1-6 is evident in the similar terminology:

> For this reason I, Paul, a prisoner for Christ Jesus on behalf of you Gentiles *(tōn ethnōn)*—assuming that you have heard of the stewardship of God's grace that was given to me for you,[2] how the

---

[1] Jer 1:4-10; Ezek 2:1-2; 3:1-4.

[2] Compare with Galatians 1:15-16: "But when he who had set me apart before I was born, and had called me through his *grace*, was pleased to reveal his Son to me, in order that I might preach him *among the Gentiles*, I did not confer with flesh and blood."

mystery was made known *(egnōristhē)* to me by revelation *(kata apokalypsin)*,[3] as I have written briefly. When you read this[4] you can perceive my insight into the mystery of Christ, which was not made known *(egnōristhē)* to the sons of men in other generations as it has now been revealed *(apekalyphthē)* to his holy apostles and prophets by the Spirit; that is, how the Gentiles are fellow heirs, members of the same body, and partakers of the promise in Christ Jesus through the gospel.

The mystery Paul is speaking of is not an ontological mystery, but rather a mystery hidden to someone who has not yet been privy to it. In this particular case, the teaching communicated by the prophets is originally a mystery known only to God who then communicated it to his prophets: "Surely the Lord God does nothing, without revealing his (secret) counsel *(sod)* to his servants the prophets. The lion has roared; who will not fear? The Lord God has spoken; who can but prophesy? Proclaim to the strongholds in Assyria, and to the strongholds in the land of Egypt, and say…" (Am 3:7-9a) In turn, when this message is consigned in "the prophetic writings" (Rom 16:26), it ceases to be a mystery to the Jews who "are entrusted with the oracles of God" (3:2). Still the same message remains a mystery to the Gentiles until it is communicated to them by Paul, who is "called to be an apostle, set apart for the gospel of God which he promised beforehand through his prophets in the holy scriptures" (1:1-2). This explication is confirmed in Romans 16:26-27 and in Ephesians 3:1-6, with both passages indicating that the mystery specifically concerns "the nations." Now that the mystery is

---

[3] Compare with Galatians 1:11-12 and 2:1: "For I would have you know, brethren, that the *gospel* which was preached by me is not man's *gospel*. For I did not receive it from man, nor was I taught it, but it came through a revelation *(di' apokalypseōs)* of Jesus Christ." "I went up by revelation *(kata apokalypsin)*; and I laid before them (but privately before those who were of repute) the *gospel* which I preach *among the Gentiles*, lest somehow I should be running or had run in vain."

[4] Compare with Galatians 1:9; 5:2; and 6:11: "As we have said before, so now I say (in writing) again." "Now I, Paul, say (in writing) to you." "See with what large letters I am writing to you with my own hand."

revealed, it ceases to be a mystery. Classical Christian teaching across the board revels in the term "mystery" in order that select "theologians" and "spiritual leaders" keep control over the people as their predecessors, the priests and kings of the scriptural Israel and Judah, did. In so doing, the leaders of Isreal and Judah fell under the judgment of God's prophets. Not so Paul. His aim is always to invite his addressees to "walk the way" as will be made clear in the remainder of this letter.[5]

What is stunning in Ephesians is that nowhere in the letter does Paul refer to himself as "slave" (*doulos*), especially in conjunction with his preaching the gospel. He refers to himself as a slave in all his preceding letters, either directly (Rom 1:1; 2 Cor 4:5; Gal 1:10), or indirectly as *oikonomos*, house manager (1 Cor 4:1-2), who is a slave in charge. What makes this even more perplexing is that Paul refers to his mission as *oikonomia*, just as he has done in 1 Corinthians 9:17, and no less than three times (Eph 1:10; 3:2, 9) two of which in this chapter. Add to this that, in the following letter to the Philippians, Paul reverts to his habit of referring to himself as slave at the outset (1:1) as he did in Romans. Even in Colossians, the only other letter where he introduces himself primarily as *diakonos* (table minister; 1:23, 25), he still refers to himself obliquely as a slave: "Tychicus will tell you all about my affairs; he is a beloved brother and faithful minister (*diakonos*) and fellow servant (*syndoulos*; co-slave, fellow slave) in the Lord." (4:7)

Ephesus was the capital city of one of the most important Eastern Roman provinces in Asia, a city that hosted the Temple of Artemis, one of the wonders of the ancient world. So, by qualifying his apostolic mission as *diakonia* (table ministry), a staple of household life, over that of *douleia* (slavery), a staple of senatorial and imperial Roman mores, Paul was reminding the Ephesians, that their new way of life, their new polity, revolved *around the scriptural God's scripturalized* (consigned *in* and *as* scripture) *teaching* that took place in their homes during table fellowship (1

---

[5] I shall elaborate on this matter in my comments at the beginning of chapter 5.

Cor 11:17-26). More importantly, on the practical level, it is during table fellowship that their behavior toward their peers is tested time and again in order to help them pass muster at God's final judgment when he will appear as ruler of the universe. God's judgment will entail potential condemnation (v.32) and be without appeal (vv.27-34), just as the Roman emperor's power over the lives of his "slaves" in the arena is without appeal. The aspect of "preliminary" judgment unto "education" (v.32) at table gatherings in the homes is enhanced by the fact that the remembrance does not include the victory of the Lord's resurrection as a prelude to his coming: "For as often as you eat this bread and drink the cup, you proclaim *the Lord's death until he comes.*" (v.26) Thus the new reality for the Ephesians is centered around the *kat' oikon ekklesia,* that is, God's imperial arena of action, and not *the church at large* as it has been constructed mentally in all theologies (Orthodox, Catholic, Lutheran, Reformed, Presbyterian, Methodist, Baptist, etc.) across the board. That is to say, there is no *universal* church that ends up bestowing divine authority to its individual congregations. Rather each and every *kat' oikon ekklesia* is "the church" so long as Paul is its *diakonos* "in *his* scriptures" (1 Pet 3:15-16). This will be confirmed later where the setting for the rules of behavior between church members is indubitably the individual Roman household (Eph 5:21-6:9).

It is indeed the "chained"—as a slave in the imperial arena would be—(*desmios;* Eph 3:1) Paul, who is the *diakonos* to whom has been revealed the mystery of God and who carries the working of God's power in our midst and world. As such, he has become the high priest of every *kat' oikon ekklesia* (Eph 1:16; see also Rom 15:15-16; Phil 2:17; Col 4:18) Note how the vocabulary of chapter 3 reprises that of chapter 1:

> He destined us in love to be his sons through Jesus Christ, according to the purpose of his will, to the praise of his glorious grace which he freely bestowed on us in the Beloved. In him we have redemption through his blood, the forgiveness of our trespasses, according to the riches of his grace which he lavished

upon us. For he has made known to us in all wisdom and insight the mystery of his will, according to his purpose which he set forth in Christ as a plan (*oikonomian*) for the fulness of time, to unite all things in him, things in heaven and things on earth. In him, according to the purpose of him who accomplishes all things according to the counsel of his will, we who first hoped in Christ have been destined and appointed to live for the praise of his glory. (1:5-12)

For this reason I, Paul, a prisoner for Christ Jesus on behalf of you Gentiles – assuming that you have heard of the stewardship (*oikonomian*) of God's grace that was given to me for you. (3:1-2)

It is through such church (*kat' oikon ekklesia*) that the manifold wisdom of the universal God is imparted to the principalities and powers in the heavenly places (3:10), that is to say, to the leaders of Rome and those of Jerusalem.[6] The corollary is that glory is rendered to God *"in the church*—a unique instance in the New Testament—and in Christ Jesus to all generations, for ever and ever" (v.21). This is against the grain since glory (Hebrew *kabod*) reflects "weightiness," and thus importance, and consequently is befitting imperial residences and majestic temples as is eminently clear from human literature as well as scripture. And since it is against the grain, it is phrased as a prayer on hope that it be so, as is evident from the final "Amen" at the end of verse 21.

The centrality of *diakonia* can be gleaned from Romans 15. In Philippians Paul does not shy from projecting his and Timothy's status of "slaves (*douloi*)" (1:1; see also Rom 1:1) onto the Christ Jesus himself (Phil 2:5): "but emptied himself, taking the form of a servant (*doulou*; slave), being born in the likeness of men." (2:7) In Romans, after having heard of Paul's ministry (*diakonia*) in 11:13, one hears of Christ as "minister" (*diakonon*; rendered as servant in RSV) to those of the circumcision (15:7) in conjunction with Paul's gospel to the Gentiles. What is significant in this regard is that this statement comes at the end of a paragraph that

---

[6] See my comments above on Eph 1 in conjunction with Col 1:16 and 2:15 (see *C-Col* 47-48, 70).

functions as a conclusion based on the lengthy chapter 14 which deals with one's behavior toward the "weaker" brother *at table fellowship*:

> We who are strong ought to bear with the failings of the weak, and not to please ourselves; let each of us please his neighbor for his good, to edify him (*pros oikodomēn* [unto edification] from the same root as *oikos* [house]). For Christ did not please himself; but, as it is written, "The reproaches of those who reproached thee fell on me." For whatever was written in former days was written for our instruction, that by steadfastness and by the encouragement of the scriptures we might have hope. May the God of steadfastness and encouragement grant you to live in such harmony with one another, in accord with Christ Jesus, that together you may with one voice glorify the God and Father of our Lord Jesus Christ. Welcome one another, therefore, as Christ has welcomed you, for the glory of God. For I tell you that Christ became a servant (*diakonon*; minister) to the circumcised to show God's truthfulness, in order to confirm the promises given to the patriarchs, and in order that the Gentiles might glorify God for his mercy. As it is written, "Therefore I will praise thee among the Gentiles, and sing to thy name." (15:1-9)

Unfortunately, instead of heeding the apostolic teaching and its premise, all Christian traditions followed, willy nilly, the "imperial" way. Just as Paul's opponents, the Jews of Jerusalem and those of Judah before them, opted for the temple of Herod over the synagogue, the Christians, in all their traditions, opted for church buildings over Paul's *kat' oikon ekklēsia* and then imagined and re-read their own fabricated "church" into all the instances of "church" in the New Testament. They did so architecturally as well as theologically. This approach became so engrained that even the tiniest Christian community devises an impressive website that functions as a (self-)magnifying lens through which the outsider perceives their "church." Put otherwise, in contravention of the prophetic and apostolic teaching, the Christians follow the tradition initiated by David and Solomon to move the scriptural God out of his movable "tent" into a stone building, thus forgetting that it is that same God who ends up destroying the stone temple. All Christian traditions give the impression that God's work (*ergon*) begins and ends with *their leitourgia* (church [building] service). The traditional Christian communities even distort the original meaning of the Pauline Roman household table fellowship—where the bread is still referred to as bread even after the words of "institution" (1 Cor 11:23-24 and 26-28)—into a sacramental meal, that is, a sacred rite. They make out of consumable bread the "life-giving substance," supplanting the "teaching" of scripture as the true "bread unto life," thus upending the meaning and function of John 6. In other words they do not take to heart that Christ "resides"—as in a house—(*katoikēsai*) among us only in so far our trust (*pisteōs*) in his words of teaching is translated into our "being rooted and grounded in (our) love (for others)" (Eph 3:17;[7] see also Gal 5:5-6). This is God's plan for us that was "rooted and grounded" all along "before the foundation of the world": "Blessed *be* the God and Father of our Lord Jesus Christ, who hath blessed us with all spiritual blessings in heavenly *places* in Christ: According as he hath chosen us in him before the foundation of the world, that we should be holy and without blame before him *in love*." (Eph 1:3-4 KJV)[8] And lest someone is tempted to use "the cunning of men" and "their craftiness in deceitful wiles"—strictly forbidden by Paul (Eph 4:14)—to transform one's community's website into a forum for an exhibition entitled "our love in action," my readers are reminded of scripture's strict rule: "But when you give alms, do not let your left hand know what your right hand is doing, so that your alms may be in secret; and your Father—before whom the Apostle bowed his knees (Eph 3:14)—who sees in secret will reward you." (Mt 6:3-4)

---

[7] See also a few verses later an iteration of the same, this time over as a request: "I therefore, a prisoner for the Lord, beg you to lead a life worthy of the calling to which you have been called, with all lowliness and meekness, with patience, *forbearing one another in love*." (Eph 4:1-2)

[8] KJV is closer to the original than RSV.

Chapter 4

Vv. 1-32 ¹Παρακαλῶ οὖν ὑμᾶς ἐγὼ ὁ δέσμιος ἐν κυρίῳ ἀξίως περιπατῆσαι τῆς κλήσεως ἧς ἐκλήθητέ ²μετὰ πάσης ταπεινοφροσύνης καὶ πραΰτητος μετὰ μακροθυμίας ἀνεχόμενοι ἀλλήλων ἐν ἀγάπῃ ³σπουδάζοντες τηρεῖν τὴν ἑνότητα τοῦ πνεύματος ἐν τῷ συνδέσμῳ τῆς εἰρήνης· ⁴Ἓν σῶμα καὶ ἓν πνεῦμά καθὼς καὶ ἐκλήθητε ἐν μιᾷ ἐλπίδι τῆς κλήσεως ὑμῶν· ⁵εἷς κύριος μία πίστις ἓν βάπτισμά ⁶εἷς θεὸς καὶ πατὴρ πάντων ὁ ἐπὶ πάντων καὶ διὰ πάντων καὶ ἐν πᾶσιν ⁷Ἑνὶ δὲ ἑκάστῳ ἡμῶν ἐδόθη ἡ χάρις κατὰ τὸ μέτρον τῆς δωρεᾶς τοῦ Χριστοῦ· ⁸διὸ λέγει· ἀναβὰς εἰς ὕψος ᾐχμαλώτευσεν αἰχμαλωσίαν ἔδωκεν δόματα τοῖς ἀνθρώποις· ⁹τὸ δὲ ἀνέβη τί ἐστιν εἰ μὴ ὅτι καὶ κατέβη εἰς τὰ κατώτερα ᾽μέρῃ᾽ τῆς γῆς· ¹⁰ὁ καταβὰς αὐτός ἐστιν καὶ ὁ ἀναβὰς ὑπεράνω πάντων τῶν οὐρανῶν ἵνα πληρώσῃ τὰ πάντά ¹¹Καὶ αὐτὸς ἔδωκεν τοὺς μὲν ἀποστόλους τοὺς δὲ προφήτας τοὺς δὲ εὐαγγελιστάς τοὺς δὲ ποιμένας καὶ διδασκάλους ¹²πρὸς τὸν καταρτισμὸν τῶν ἁγίων εἰς ἔργον διακονίας εἰς οἰκοδομὴν τοῦ σώματος τοῦ Χριστοῦ ¹³μέχρι καταντήσωμεν οἱ πάντες εἰς τὴν ἑνότητα τῆς πίστεως καὶ τῆς ἐπιγνώσεως τοῦ υἱοῦ τοῦ θεοῦ εἰς ἄνδρα τέλειόν εἰς μέτρον ἡλικίας τοῦ πληρώματος τοῦ Χριστοῦ ¹⁴ἵνα μηκέτι ὦμεν νήπιοί κλυδωνιζόμενοι καὶ περιφερόμενοι παντὶ ἀνέμῳ τῆς διδασκαλίας ἐν τῇ κυβείᾳ τῶν ἀνθρώπων ἐν πανουργίᾳ πρὸς τὴν μεθοδείαν τῆς πλάνης ¹⁵ἀληθεύοντες δὲ ἐν ἀγάπῃ αὐξήσωμεν εἰς αὐτὸν τὰ πάντά ὅς ἐστιν ἡ κεφαλή Χριστός ¹⁶ἐξ οὗ πᾶν τὸ σῶμα συναρμολογούμενον καὶ συμβιβαζόμενον διὰ πάσης ἁφῆς τῆς ἐπιχορηγίας κατ᾽ ἐνέργειαν ἐν μέτρῳ ἑνὸς ἑκάστου μέρους τὴν αὔξησιν τοῦ σώματος ποιεῖται εἰς οἰκοδομὴν ἑαυτοῦ ἐν ἀγάπῃ ¹⁷Τοῦτο οὖν λέγω καὶ μαρτύρομαι ἐν κυρίῳ μηκέτι ὑμᾶς περιπατεῖν καθὼς καὶ τὰ ἔθνη περιπατεῖ ἐν ματαιότητι τοῦ νοὸς αὐτῶν ¹⁸ἐσκοτωμένοι τῇ διανοίᾳ ὄντες ἀπηλλοτριωμένοι τῆς ζωῆς τοῦ θεοῦ διὰ τὴν ἄγνοιαν τὴν οὖσαν ἐν αὐτοῖς

79

διὰ τὴν πώρωσιν τῆς καρδίας αὐτῶν ¹⁹οἵτινες ἀπηλγηκότες ἑαυτοὺς παρέδωκαν τῇ ἀσελγείᾳ εἰς ἐργασίαν ἀκαθαρσίας πάσης ἐν πλεονεξίᾳ ²⁰ὑμεῖς δὲ οὐχ οὕτως ἐμάθετε τὸν Χριστόν ²¹εἴ γε αὐτὸν ἠκούσατε καὶ ἐν αὐτῷ ἐδιδάχθητέ καθώς ἐστιν ἀλήθεια ἐν τῷ Ἰησοῦ ²²ἀποθέσθαι ὑμᾶς κατὰ τὴν προτέραν ἀναστροφὴν τὸν παλαιὸν ἄνθρωπον τὸν φθειρόμενον κατὰ τὰς ἐπιθυμίας τῆς ἀπάτης ²³ἀνανεοῦσθαι δὲ τῷ πνεύματι τοῦ νοὸς ὑμῶν ²⁴καὶ ἐνδύσασθαι τὸν καινὸν ἄνθρωπον τὸν κατὰ θεὸν κτισθέντα ἐν δικαιοσύνῃ καὶ ὁσιότητι τῆς ἀληθείας ²⁵Διὸ ἀποθέμενοι τὸ ψεῦδος λαλεῖτε ἀλήθειαν ἕκαστος μετὰ τοῦ πλησίον αὐτοῦ ὅτι ἐσμὲν ἀλλήλων μέλη ²⁶ὀργίζεσθε καὶ μὴ ἁμαρτάνετε· ὁ ἥλιος μὴ ἐπιδυέτω ἐπὶ τῷ παροργισμῷ ὑμῶν ²⁷μηδὲ δίδοτε τόπον τῷ διαβόλῳ ²⁸ὁ κλέπτων μηκέτι κλεπτέτω· μᾶλλον δὲ κοπιάτω ἐργαζόμενος ταῖς ἰδίαις χερσὶν τὸ ἀγαθόν ἵνα ἔχῃ μεταδιδόναι τῷ χρείαν ἔχοντι ²⁹πᾶς λόγος σαπρὸς ἐκ τοῦ στόματος ὑμῶν μὴ ἐκπορευέσθω· ἀλλὰ εἴ τις ἀγαθὸς πρὸς οἰκοδομὴν τῆς χρείας ἵνα δῷ χάριν τοῖς ἀκούουσιν ³⁰καὶ μὴ λυπεῖτε τὸ πνεῦμα τὸ ἅγιον τοῦ θεοῦ ἐν ᾧ ἐσφραγίσθητε εἰς ἡμέραν ἀπολυτρώσεως ³¹πᾶσα πικρία καὶ θυμὸς καὶ ὀργὴ καὶ κραυγὴ καὶ βλασφημία ἀρθήτω ἀφ᾽ ὑμῶν σὺν πάσῃ κακίᾳ ³²γίνεσθε δὲ εἰς ἀλλήλους χρηστοί εὔσπλαγχνοι χαριζόμενοι ἑαυτοῖς καθὼς καὶ ὁ θεὸς ἐν Χριστῷ ἐχαρίσατο ὑμῖν

¹I therefore, a prisoner for the Lord, beg you to lead a life worthy of the calling to which you have been called, ²with all lowliness and meekness, with patience, forbearing one another in love, ³eager to maintain the unity of the Spirit in the bond of peace. ⁴There is one body and one Spirit, just as you were called to the one hope that belongs to your call, ⁵one Lord, one faith, one baptism, ⁶one God and Father of us all, who is above all and through all and in all. ⁷But grace was given to each of us according to the measure of Christ's gift. ⁸Therefore it is said, "When he ascended on high he led a host of captives, and he gave gifts to men." ⁹(In saying,

"He ascended," what does it mean but that he had also descended into the lower parts of the earth? [10] He who descended is he who also ascended far above all the heavens, that he might fill all things.) [11] And his gifts were that some should be apostles, some prophets, some evangelists, some pastors and teachers, [12] to equip the saints for the work of ministry, for building up the body of Christ, [13] until we all attain to the unity of the faith and of the knowledge of the Son of God, to mature manhood, to the measure of the stature of the fulness of Christ; [14] so that we may no longer be children, tossed to and fro and carried about with every wind of doctrine, by the cunning of men, by their craftiness in deceitful wiles. [15] Rather, speaking the truth in love, we are to grow up in every way into him who is the head, into Christ, [16] from whom the whole body, joined and knit together by every joint with which it is supplied, when each part is working properly, makes bodily growth and upbuilds itself in love. [17] Now this I affirm and testify in the Lord, that you must no longer live as the Gentiles do, in the futility of their minds; [18] they are darkened in their understanding, alienated from the life of God because of the ignorance that is in them, due to their hardness of heart; [19] they have become callous and have given themselves up to licentiousness, greedy to practice every kind of uncleanness. [20] You did not so learn Christ!— [21] assuming that you have heard about him and were taught in him, as the truth is in Jesus. [22] Put off your old nature which belongs to your former manner of life and is corrupt through deceitful lusts, [23] and be renewed in the spirit of your minds, [24] and put on the new nature, created after the likeness of God in true righteousness and holiness. [25] Therefore, putting away falsehood, let every one speak the truth with his neighbor, for we are members one of another. [26] Be angry but do not sin; do not let the sun go down on your anger, [27] and give no opportunity to the devil. [28] Let the thief no longer steal, but rather let him labor, doing honest work with his hands, so that he may be able to give to those in need. [29] Let no evil talk come out of your mouths, but only such as is good for edifying, as fits the occasion, that it may impart grace to those who hear. [30] And do not grieve the Holy Spirit of God, in whom you were sealed for the day of redemption. [31] Let all bitterness and wrath and anger and clamor and slander be put away from you, with all malice, [32] and be kind to one another, tenderhearted, forgiving one another, as God in Christ forgave you.

Before proceeding to chapter 5 where Paul seals his vision of the church "according" (*kata*) to a Roman household, he sums up his entire teaching concerning the "rule of life" in his churches in the magisterial compendium of chapter 4. In it he brings together pertinent, if not central, imageries not only from Ephesians 1-3, but also from the rest of the Pauline corpus, especially the letters that precede Ephesians in the canon. It is a literary tour de force when the well-knit totality of the major imageries is bracketed between the mention of "love" (v.2), with which he concluded chapter 3, and a detailed coverage of the factual expression of this love (4:25-32) reminiscent of Galatians 5:22-23 (and 1 Corinthians 13). This is befitting since the Galatians reference is preceded with and is a commentary on the statement in 5:14: "For the whole law is fulfilled in one word, 'You shall love your neighbor as yourself.'" Still, it is the phraseology that confirms the immediacy of the link between the two:

I therefore, a prisoner for the Lord, beg you to *lead a life* (*peripatēsai*; walk) worthy of the calling to which you have been called, with all lowliness and *meekness* (*praytētos*), with *patience*, forbearing one another in *love*, eager to maintain the unity of the *Spirit* in the bond of *peace*. (Eph 4:1-3)

But I say, *walk* (*peripateite*) by the *Spirit*, and do not gratify the desires of the flesh … But the fruit of the *Spirit* is *love*, joy, *peace*, *patience*, kindness, goodness, faithfulness, *gentleness* (*praytēs*), self-control; against such there is no law. (Gal 5:16, 22-23)

The mention of "lowliness" (*tapeinophrosynēs*) in conjunction with "meekness" and "patience" in Ephesians 4:2 is introduced in view of vv.8-10, reflecting Christ's "ascension" to glory as a result of his having "descended," and is a clear reflection of Philippians 2:11 which is preceded by:

complete my joy by being of the same mind, having the same *love*, being in full accord and of one mind. Do nothing from selfishness or conceit, but in humility (*tapeinophrosynē*) count others better than yourselves. (vv.2-3)

The reference to the "gift (*dōreas*) according to the measure (*metron*)" (Eph 4:7) prepares for the different kinds of "gifts" in v.11.[1] In so doing Paul points to both Romans and 1 Corinthians:

For by the grace given to me I bid every one among you not to think of himself more highly than he ought to think, but to think with sober judgment, each according to the measure of faith which God has assigned him. For as in one body we have many members, and all the members do not have the same function, so we, though many, are one body in Christ, and individually members one of another. Having gifts that differ according to the grace given to us, let us use them: if prophecy, in proportion to our faith; if service, in our serving; he who teaches, in his teaching; he who exhorts, in his exhortation; he who contributes, in liberality; he who gives aid, with zeal; he who does acts of mercy, with cheerfulness. Let love be genuine; hate what is evil, hold fast to what is good; love one another with brotherly affection; outdo one another in showing honor. (Rom 12:3-10)

Now you are the body of Christ and individually members of it. And God has appointed in the church first apostles, second prophets, third teachers, then workers of miracles, then healers, helpers, administrators, speakers in various kinds of tongues. Are all apostles? Are all prophets? Are all teachers? Do all work miracles? Do all possess gifts of healing? Do all speak with tongues? Do all interpret? But earnestly desire the higher gifts. And I will show you a still more excellent way. (1 Cor 12:27-31)

If I speak in the tongues of men and of angels, but have not love, I am a noisy gong or a clanging cymbal. And if I have prophetic powers, and understand all mysteries and all knowledge, and if I have all faith, so as to remove mountains, but have not love, I am nothing. If I give away all I have, and if I deliver my body to be burned, but have not love, I gain nothing. (13:1-3)

Ephesians 4:12 is ingenious in how it weaves together this epistle and 1 Corinthians. After having referred in Ephesians 4:11 to a list taken from 1 Corinthians 12, Paul ends up with "building

---

[1] The original for "And his gifts were that some should be" is "And he gave (*edoken*, from the same root as *dōreas*) as."

the body"—also from 1 Corinthians 12—in conjunction with "ministry" (*diakonias*) which is a staple of Ephesians. However, at the beginning of 1 Corinthians 12 one hears the mention of "ministries" (*diakoniais*) in conjunction with the Spirit that is the source of the various "gifts": "Now there are varieties of gifts (*kharismatōn*), but the same Spirit; and there are varieties of service (*diakoniōn*; ministries), but the same Lord." (vv.4-5) Add to this that in both epistles the "ministries" of the individuals are rooted in the "ministerial activity" (*diakonia*) of the Apostle himself: in both cases one hears first of Paul the *diakonos* (Eph 3:7; 1 Cor 3:5) and then of the *diakonia* of the individual members of his churches (Eph 4:12; 1 Cor 12:5).

Ephesians 4:12 is also linked with 2 Corinthians through the use of *pros ton katartismon* (to equip; unto the equipment of), a root used rarely in the Pauline writings, found here in Ephesians and twice in 2 Corinthians 13:

> For we are glad when we are weak and you are strong. What we pray for is your improvement (*katartisin*). I write this while I am away from you, in order that when I come I may not have to be severe in my use of the authority which the Lord has given me *for building up* (*eis oikodomēn*) and not for tearing down. Finally, brethren, farewell. Mend your ways (*katartizesthe*), heed my appeal, agree with one another, live in *peace*, and the God of love and peace will be with you. (vv.9-11).

The link is enhanced through the occurrence of "for building up" in v.10 and "peace" in v.11 that are found in Ephesians 4: "eager to maintain the unity of the Spirit in the bond of *peace* (v.3) … to equip the saints for the work of ministry, *for building up* (*eis oikodomēn*) the body of Christ (v.12)."

Paul ends with the lengthy passage (Eph 4:15-22) that starts with the admonition "Rather, *speaking the truth* (*alēthevontes*) in love, we are to grow up in every way into him who is the head, into Christ." It is only befitting that Paul would wrap up the corpus of his teaching in his "compendium" letter addressed obliquely to all his churches[2] with a direct reference to Galatians, the blue print of the entire New Testament literature. The verb *alēthevō* (speak truthfully) occurs one other time in the New Testament, in Galatians, in a context where Paul is referring to his boundless love for his addressees: "What has become of the satisfaction you felt? For I bear you witness that, if possible, you would have plucked out your eyes and given them to me. Have I then become your enemy by *telling* you *the truth* (*alēthevōn*)?" (4:15-16) Given the totality of the argument in Galatians, the "truth" communicated through the verb *alēthevō* is "the truth of the gospel" (2:5 and 14)— or simply "the truth" (5:7)—for whose sake Paul braved the "pillars" both in Jerusalem and at Antioch (2:1-14). This same phraseology was heard earlier in Ephesians: "In him you also, who have heard *the word of truth, the gospel* of your salvation, and have believed in him, were sealed with the promised Holy Spirit." (1:13) And the "gospel" is nothing other than the Pauline teaching without "the cunning of men" and "their craftiness in deceitful wiles" (Eph 4:14), that is, "the tradition of men" (Col 2:8) which Paul counteracted by scripturalizing his writ to his churches and their leaders (4:16).[3] Thus the "gospel" is tantamount to Paul's letters as confirmed in Galatians:

> But even if we, or an angel from heaven, should preach to you a gospel contrary to that which we preached to you, let him be accursed. As we have said before, so *now I say* (in this letter I am penning) again, If any one is preaching to you a gospel contrary to that which you received, let him be accursed. (1:8-9)

> *Now I*, Paul, *say* (in this letter I am penning) to you that if you receive circumcision, Christ will be of no advantage to you. (5:2)

---

[2] See Introduction.

[3] See my comments in *C-Col* 103.

See with what large letters *I am writing* to you with my own hand.
(6:11)4

Consequently his statement, "You did not so learn Christ!—
assuming that you have heard about him and were taught in him,
as the truth is in Jesus" (Eph 4:20-21), should be heard as saying,
"You did not so learn Christ!—assuming that you have heard
(**from me**) about him and were taught (**by me**) in him, as *the truth*
is in Jesus (**as preached to you by me**)" (1:13).

As I consistently keep reminding my hearers and readers, we
have to teach the "words" of Paul and his school, just as Jeremiah
regurgitated the "words" that the Lord had put in his (Jeremiah's)
mouth (Jer 1 and 36). Our "commentating" sermons and our
"commentaries" are simply "our take" on the divine and apostolic
already written words that are to be read aloud to the congregation.[5]
"Our take," at best, makes God look "complicated" and, at worst,
needs a Hermes like the deities of the nations. The divine message
is readily transparent to the ear, witness the reaction of King
Jehoiakim (Jer 36:23) and that of the scribes and the chief priests
(Lk 20:19). Our sermons and commentaries should simply
amount to explaining the original meaning of the words in order
for the hearers to be faced with the "intention of the story line,"
and to be judged in order to undergo correction so that they not
end up condemned: "But if we judged ourselves truly, we should
not be judged. But when we are judged by the Lord, we are
chastened so that we may not be condemned along with the
world." (1 Cor 11:31-32) This is God's attitude in scripture after
(if not before) all:

---

[4] In turn this explains why his disciple titled his writ "gospel," "The beginning of the
gospel of Jesus Christ, the Son of God" (Mk 1:1), copying the exact words of his teacher:
"And you Philippians yourselves know that in the beginning of the gospel, when I left
Macedonia, no church entered into partnership with me in giving and receiving except
you only." (Phil 4:15)
[5] And "our take" is after all nothing else save "our thoughts" regarding the "matter"
(*dabar*) which are, more often than not, *not* in line with "God's thoughts" (Is 55:8-9).

> Have I any pleasure in the death of the wicked, says the Lord God, and not rather that he should turn from his way and live? (Ezek 18:23)

> For I have no pleasure in the death of any one, says the Lord God; so turn, and live. (18:32)

> As I live, says the Lord, I have no pleasure in the death of the wicked, but that the wicked turn from his way and live; turn back, turn back from your evil ways; for why will you die, O house of Israel? (33:11)

It is rather we, using "the cunning of men" and "their craftiness in deceitful wiles," who either desire the death of the wicked or want to overbid God in mercy by "cajoling" our hearers in proclaiming "peace" when he himself has not proclaimed it (Jer 6:14; 8:11, 15; 14:19; Ezek 13:10, 16). In conjunction with this, revisiting the beginning of Ephesians 4 shows how it encapsulates the message of the entire chapter, or at least determines its mindset.

> I therefore, a prisoner (*desmios*; chained, in chains) for the Lord, beg you to lead a life worthy of the calling to which you have been called, with all lowliness and meekness, with patience, forbearing one another in love, eager to maintain the unity of the Spirit in the bond (*syndesmō*; chain, chaining) of peace. (vv.1-3)

Since Paul already introduced himself as *desmios* in 3:1, the repeat in 4:1 is then obviously intentional in that it functions as an attention getter in preparation of his use of *syndesmos* at the end of the sentence.

Chapter 5

Vv. 1-20 ¹Γίνεσθε οὖν μιμηταὶ τοῦ θεοῦ ὡς τέκνα ἀγαπητὰ ²καὶ περιπατεῖτε ἐν ἀγάπῃ καθὼς καὶ ὁ Χριστὸς ἠγάπησεν ἡμᾶς καὶ παρέδωκεν ἑαυτὸν ὑπὲρ ἡμῶν προσφορὰν καὶ θυσίαν τῷ θεῷ εἰς ὀσμὴν εὐωδίας· ³Πορνεία δὲ καὶ ἀκαθαρσία πᾶσα ἢ πλεονεξία μηδὲ ὀνομαζέσθω ἐν ὑμῖν καθὼς πρέπει ἁγίοις· ⁴καὶ αἰσχρότης καὶ μωρολογία ἢ εὐτραπελία ἃ οὐκ ἀνῆκεν ἀλλὰ μᾶλλον εὐχαριστία· ⁵τοῦτο γὰρ ἴστε γινώσκοντες ὅτι πᾶς πόρνος ἢ ἀκάθαρτος ἢ πλεονέκτης ὅ ἐστιν εἰδωλολάτρης οὐκ ἔχει κληρονομίαν ἐν τῇ βασιλείᾳ τοῦ Χριστοῦ καὶ θεοῦ· ⁶Μηδεὶς ὑμᾶς ἀπατάτω κενοῖς λόγοις· διὰ ταῦτα γὰρ ἔρχεται ἡ ὀργὴ τοῦ θεοῦ ἐπὶ τοὺς υἱοὺς τῆς ἀπειθείας· ⁷μὴ οὖν γίνεσθε συμμέτοχοι αὐτῶν· ⁸ἦτε γάρ ποτε σκότος νῦν δὲ φῶς ἐν κυρίῳ· ὡς τέκνα φωτὸς περιπατεῖτε ⁹ὁ γὰρ καρπὸς τοῦ φωτὸς ἐν πάσῃ ἀγαθωσύνῃ καὶ δικαιοσύνῃ καὶ ἀληθείᾳ ¹⁰δοκιμάζοντες τί ἐστιν εὐάρεστον τῷ κυρίῳ· ¹¹καὶ μὴ συγκοινωνεῖτε τοῖς ἔργοις τοῖς ἀκάρποις τοῦ σκότους μᾶλλον δὲ καὶ ἐλέγχετε· ¹²τὰ γὰρ κρυφῇ γινόμενα ὑπ' αὐτῶν αἰσχρόν ἐστιν καὶ λέγειν· ¹³τὰ δὲ πάντα ἐλεγχόμενα ὑπὸ τοῦ φωτὸς φανεροῦται· ¹⁴πᾶν γὰρ τὸ φανερούμενον φῶς ἐστιν· διὸ λέγει· ἔγειρε ὁ καθεύδων καὶ ἀνάστα ἐκ τῶν νεκρῶν καὶ ἐπιφαύσει σοι ὁ Χριστός· ¹⁵Βλέπετε οὖν ἀκριβῶς πῶς περιπατεῖτε μὴ ὡς ἄσοφοι ἀλλ' ὡς σοφοί ¹⁶ἐξαγοραζόμενοι τὸν καιρόν ὅτι αἱ ἡμέραι πονηραί εἰσιν· ¹⁷διὰ τοῦτο μὴ γίνεσθε ἄφρονες ἀλλὰ συνίετε τί τὸ θέλημα τοῦ κυρίου· ¹⁸καὶ μὴ μεθύσκεσθε οἴνῳ ἐν ᾧ ἐστιν ἀσωτία ἀλλὰ πληροῦσθε ἐν πνεύματι ¹⁹λαλοῦντες ἑαυτοῖς ἐν ψαλμοῖς καὶ ὕμνοις καὶ ᾠδαῖς πνευματικαῖς ᾄδοντες καὶ ψάλλοντες τῇ καρδίᾳ ὑμῶν τῷ κυρίῳ· ²⁰εὐχαριστοῦντες πάντοτε ὑπὲρ πάντων ἐν ὀνόματι τοῦ κυρίου ἡμῶν Ἰησοῦ Χριστοῦ τῷ θεῷ καὶ πατρί·

[1]Therefore be imitators of God, as beloved children. [2]And walk in love, as Christ loved us and gave himself up for us, a fragrant offering and sacrifice to God. [3]But fornication and all impurity or covetousness must not even be named among you, as is fitting among saints. [4]Let there be no filthiness, nor silly talk, nor levity, which are not fitting; but instead let there be thanksgiving. [5]Be sure of this, that no fornicator or impure man, or one who is covetous (that is, an idolater), has any inheritance in the kingdom of Christ and of God. [6]Let no one deceive you with empty words, for it is because of these things that the wrath of God comes upon the sons of disobedience. [7]Therefore do not associate with them, [8]for once you were darkness, but now you are light in the Lord; walk as children of light [9](for the fruit of light is found in all that is good and right and true), [10]and try to learn what is pleasing to the Lord. [11]Take no part in the unfruitful works of darkness, but instead expose them. [12]For it is a shame even to speak of the things that they do in secret; [13]but when anything is exposed by the light it becomes visible, for anything that becomes visible is light. [14]Therefore it is said, "Awake, O sleeper, and arise from the dead, and Christ shall give you light." [15]Look carefully then how you walk, not as unwise men but as wise, [16]making the most of the time, because the days are evil. [17]Therefore do not be foolish, but understand what the will of the Lord is. [18]And do not get drunk with wine, for that is debauchery; but be filled with the Spirit, [19]addressing one another in psalms and hymns and spiritual songs, singing and making melody to the Lord with all your heart, [20]always and for everything giving thanks in the name of our Lord Jesus Christ to God the Father.

The overarching topic of chapters 4 and 5—indeed of the entire letter—is bracketed within love (1:5 and the ending 6:24).[1] In this endeavor, it is Christ who is given as the example to follow (5:2), yet Paul is asking the hearers at the outset to imitate God as children would their father (5:1). This is all the more striking in that imitation of God is unique in Paul who, elsewhere, requires of his hearers to imitate him (1 Cor 4:16; 1 Thess 1:6) and, though him, Christ (1 Cor 11:1). Imitating God makes sense

---

[1] Love is mentioned twice in 6:24, a unique instance in the Pauline corpus.

when one considers that the entire epistle is anchored in the starting statement:

> Blessed be the God and Father of our Lord Jesus Christ, who has blessed us in Christ with every spiritual blessing in the heavenly places, even as he chose us in him before the foundation of the world, that we should be holy and blameless before him. He destined us in love to be his sons through Jesus Christ, according to the purpose of his will, to the praise of his glorious grace which he freely bestowed on us in the Beloved. (Eph 1:3-6)

The movement originates from the one who is "the God and Father" of Jesus Christ, who blesses us in what he wrought through Christ for us to be his sons (children) according to his will so that we ultimately be found holy and blameless before him (God). This, in turn, explains the Deuteronomy style of Ephesians that reminds us at every turn of the dictates of his will.

Ephesians is woven right up to its end with and around "many and various admonitions," just as "God spoke of old many and various ways to our fathers by the prophets" (Heb 1:1). God's "many and various ways" sound as repetitive as those witnessed in the Latter Prophets. The highest level of repetitiveness in the Old Testament is found in Deuteronomy, which is a repeat of Exodus. It "recapitulates" (*anakephalaiōsasthai* [Eph 1:10]) the Law of Exodus through the stratagem of drilling into the ears unto boredom[2] the same basic message repeated ad nauseam. Moreover, not only is one to hear, but one must actually *do what one is hearing*. I am asking the indulgence of my readers, who in our civilization are used to saying "enough is enough" once the message has been clearly conveyed, to undergo what the original hearers went through at Mount Nebo, after a trek of forty years in the wilderness *after* having heard the same message forty years earlier at Mount Horeb (And Moses summoned all Israel, and said to them, "Hear, O Israel, the statutes and the ordinances which I speak in your hearing this day, and you shall learn them and be

---

[2] Pun intended since "drill" and "bore" have the same connotation, if not meaning.

careful to do them. The Lord our God made a covenant with us in Horeb. Not with our fathers did the Lord make this covenant, but with us, who are all of us here alive this day [Deut 5:1-3]):

And now, O Israel, give heed to the statutes and the ordinances which I teach you, and do them; that you may live, and go in and take possession of the land which the Lord, the God of your fathers, gives you. (4:1)

Behold, I have taught you statutes and ordinances, as the Lord my God commanded me, that you should do them in the land which you are entering to take possession of it. (4:5)

Keep them and do them. (4:6)

And the Lord commanded me at that time to teach you statutes and ordinances, that you might do them in the land which you are going over to possess. (4:14)

Now this is the commandment, the statutes and the ordinances which the Lord your God commanded me to teach you, that you may do them in the land to which you are going over, to possess it. (6:1)

Hear therefore, O Israel, and be careful to do them; that it may go well with you, and that you may multiply greatly, as the Lord, the God of your fathers, has promised you, in a land flowing with milk and honey. (6:3)

And because you hearken to these ordinances, and keep and do them, the Lord your God will keep with you the covenant and the steadfast love which he swore to your fathers to keep. (7:12)

Take heed, in an attack of leprosy, to be very careful to do according to all that the Levitical priests shall direct you; as I commanded them, so you shall be careful to do. (24:8)

This day the Lord your God commands you to do these statutes and ordinances; you shall therefore be careful to do them with all your heart and with all your soul. (26:16)

And the Lord will make you the head, and not the tail; and you shall tend upward only, and not downward; if you obey the commandments of the Lord your God, which I command you this day, being careful to do them. (28:13)

He said to them, "Lay to heart all the words which I enjoin upon you this day, that you may command them to your children, that they may be careful to do all the words of this law." (32:46)

Since Ephesians functions as the compendium of the Pauline corpus and its setting is the "fullness of time" (1:10), it stands to reason that it was conceived à la Deuteronomy just before the passage into the "earth of rest," especially in view of what we hear in Hebrews:

For if Joshua (*Iēsous*) had given them rest, God would not speak later of another day. So then, there remains a sabbath rest for the people of God; for whoever enters God's rest also ceases from his labors as God did from his. Let us therefore strive to enter that rest, *that no one fall by the same sort of disobedience...* Since then we have a great high priest who has passed through the heavens, Jesus (*Iēsoun*), the Son of God, let us hold fast our confession. (4:8-11, 14)[3]

It is worthwhile to point out the ingenuity of the phraseology in the opening of Ephesians 5 that looks back as well as forward, thus intimately linking chapters 4 and 5 into a whole:

Therefore be imitators of God, as beloved children. And walk in love, as Christ loved us and gave himself up for us, a fragrant offering and sacrifice to God. (5:1-2)

Since Ephesians 1:3-6 is practically beyond the immediate horizon of the recipients, the start of chapter 5 has been prepared for through a bridge half way between the two, i.e., in the middle of chapter 3. There Paul introduces himself as "another" Christ to imitate[4] in that he suffered for the sake of the Ephesians (3:13), which is precisely the reason (3:14a) that he bows his knees to the

---

[3] See my comments in *C-Heb* 75.

[4] As in 1 Cor 11:1.

"Father" (v.14b) in whom originates every *patria*, which denotes fatherhood as well as family around the paterfamilias (v.15). The latter is unequivocally on Paul's mind through his use of *tekna* (children; 5:1) that looks ahead to the following *tekna* who are asked to "walk" in God's light (5:8) and, more importantly, beyond that, to the *tekna* of 6:1 and 4 in conjunction with the lengthy passage concerning the manner of "walking" for each member of the Roman *familia*—household— (5:21-6:9), a section that is vintage Ephesians. Even, for an attentive ear, this "seeping" down from Christ, and beyond Paul himself, to even regular members of a household is detectable in the phrase "a fragrant offering (*osmēn evōdias*) and sacrifice (*thysian*) to God (*tō Theō*)" used here of Christ (5:2b) since the exactly same phrase describes the action of the Philippians toward Paul: "I have received full payment, and more; I am filled, having received from Epaphroditus the gifts you sent, a fragrant offering (*osmēn evōdias*), a sacrifice (*thysian*) acceptable and pleasing to God (*tō Theō*)." (Phil 4:18)

Listening even for the first time to the content of Ephesians 5:3-20 one cannot miss the fact that it is a compendium of the Pauline teaching. Verses 3-5 recall 1 Corinthians 6:9-10 and Galatians 5:19-21. The opposition between light and darkness in conjunction with the kind of actions related to each (Ephesians 5:7-18) is found both in Romans 13:11-13 and 1 Thessalonians 5:5-10. Even the admonition "making the most of (*exagorazomenoi*; redeeming) the time, because the days are evil" (Ephesians 5:16) in conjunction with the behavior connected with light and darkness seems to reflect the closeness of the end time and judgment spoken of in Romans 13:11 and 1 Thessalonians 5:1-4. Finally the entreaty of "addressing one another in psalms and hymns and spiritual songs, singing and making melody to the Lord with all your heart, always and for everything giving thanks in the name of our Lord Jesus Christ to God the Father" (Eph 5:19-20) occurs almost verbatim in Colossians 3:16: "Let the word of Christ dwell in you richly, teach and admonish one another in all wisdom, and sing psalms and hymns and spiritual songs with thankfulness in your hearts to God." Application of this only makes sense within the house table fellowship setting, and thus eases the movement into the immediately following lengthy section regarding the house rules of conduct (5:21-6:9).

Vv. 21-33 ²¹Ὑποτασσόμενοι ἀλλήλοις ἐν φόβῳ Χριστοῦ ²²αἱ γυναῖκες τοῖς ἰδίοις ἀνδράσιν ὡς τῷ κυρίῳ ²³ὅτι ἀνήρ ἐστιν κεφαλὴ τῆς γυναικὸς ὡς καὶ ὁ Χριστὸς κεφαλὴ τῆς ἐκκλησίας αὐτὸς σωτὴρ τοῦ σώματος· ²⁴ἀλλὰ ὡς ἡ ἐκκλησία ὑποτάσσεται τῷ Χριστῷ οὕτως καὶ αἱ γυναῖκες τοῖς ἀνδράσιν ἐν παντί ²⁵Οἱ ἄνδρες ἀγαπᾶτε τὰς γυναῖκας καθὼς καὶ ὁ Χριστὸς ἠγάπησεν τὴν ἐκκλησίαν καὶ ἑαυτὸν παρέδωκεν ὑπὲρ αὐτῆς ²⁶ἵνα αὐτὴν ἁγιάσῃ καθαρίσας τῷ λουτρῷ τοῦ ὕδατος ἐν ῥήματί ²⁷ἵνα παραστήσῃ αὐτὸς ἑαυτῷ ἔνδοξον τὴν ἐκκλησίαν μὴ ἔχουσαν σπίλον ἢ ῥυτίδα ἤ τι τῶν τοιούτων ἀλλ᾽ ἵνα ᾖ ἁγία καὶ ἄμωμος ²⁸οὕτως ὀφείλουσιν ͵καὶ΅ οἱ ἄνδρες ἀγαπᾶν τὰς ἑαυτῶν γυναῖκας ὡς τὰ ἑαυτῶν σώματα· ὁ ἀγαπῶν τὴν ἑαυτοῦ γυναῖκα ἑαυτὸν ἀγαπᾷ· ²⁹Οὐδεὶς γάρ ποτε τὴν ἑαυτοῦ σάρκα ἐμίσησεν ἀλλὰ ἐκτρέφει καὶ θάλπει αὐτήν καθὼς καὶ ὁ Χριστὸς τὴν ἐκκλησίαν ³⁰ὅτι μέλη ἐσμὲν τοῦ σώματος αὐτοῦ ³¹ἀντὶ τούτου καταλείψει ἄνθρωπος ͵τὸν΅ πατέρα καὶ ͵τὴν΅ μητέρα καὶ προσκολληθήσεται πρὸς τὴν γυναῖκα αὐτοῦ καὶ ἔσονται οἱ δύο εἰς σάρκα μίαν ³²τὸ μυστήριον τοῦτο μέγα ἐστίν· ἐγὼ δὲ λέγω εἰς Χριστὸν καὶ εἰς τὴν ἐκκλησίαν ³³πλὴν καὶ ὑμεῖς οἱ καθ᾽ ἕνα ἕκαστος τὴν ἑαυτοῦ γυναῖκα οὕτως ἀγαπάτω ὡς ἑαυτόν ἡ δὲ γυνὴ ἵνα φοβῆται τὸν ἄνδρα

6:1-9 ¹Τὰ τέκνα ὑπακούετε τοῖς γονεῦσιν ὑμῶν ͵ἐν΅ κυρίῳ· τοῦτο γάρ ἐστιν δίκαιον ²τίμα τὸν πατέρα σου καὶ τὴν μητέρα ἥτις ἐστὶν ἐντολὴ πρώτη ἐν ἐπαγγελίᾳ ³ἵνα εὖ σοι γένηται καὶ ἔσῃ μακροχρόνιος ἐπὶ τῆς γῆς ⁴Καὶ οἱ πατέρες μὴ παροργίζετε τὰ τέκνα ὑμῶν ἀλλὰ ἐκτρέφετε αὐτὰ ἐν παιδείᾳ καὶ νουθεσίᾳ κυρίου ⁵Οἱ δοῦλοι ὑπακούετε τοῖς

κατὰ σάρκα κυρίοις μετὰ φόβου καὶ τρόμου ἐν ἁπλότητι
τῆς καρδίας ὑμῶν ὡς τῷ Χριστῷ ⁶μὴ κατ᾽ ὀφθαλμοδουλίαν
ὡς ἀνθρωπάρεσκοι ἀλλ᾽ ὡς δοῦλοι Χριστοῦ ποιοῦντες τὸ
θέλημα τοῦ θεοῦ ἐκ ψυχῆς ⁷μετ᾽ εὐνοίας δουλεύοντες ὡς
τῷ κυρίῳ καὶ οὐκ ἀνθρώποις ⁸εἰδότες ὅτι ἕκαστος ἐάν τι
ποιήσῃ ἀγαθόν τοῦτο κομίσεται παρὰ κυρίου εἴτε δοῦλος
εἴτε ἐλεύθερος ⁹Καὶ οἱ κύριοί τὰ αὐτὰ ποιεῖτε πρὸς αὐτούς
ἀνιέντες τὴν ἀπειλήν εἰδότες ὅτι καὶ αὐτῶν καὶ ὑμῶν ὁ
κύριός ἐστιν ἐν οὐρανοῖς καὶ προσωπολημψία οὐκ ἔστιν
παρ᾽ αὐτῷ

²¹*Be subject to one another out of reverence for Christ.* ²²*Wives, be subject
to your husbands, as to the Lord.* ²³*For the husband is the head of the
wife as Christ is the head of the church, his body, and is himself its Savior.*
²⁴*As the church is subject to Christ, so let wives also be subject in
everything to their husbands.* ²⁵*Husbands, love your wives, as Christ loved
the church and gave himself up for her,* ²⁶*that he might sanctify her, having
cleansed her by the washing of water with the word,* ²⁷*that he might present
the church to himself in splendor, without spot or wrinkle or any such
thing, that she might be holy and without blemish.* ²⁸*Even so husbands
should love their wives as their own bodies. He who loves his wife loves
himself.* ²⁹*For no man ever hates his own flesh, but nourishes and
cherishes it, as Christ does the church,* ³⁰*because we are members of his
body.* ³¹*"For this reason a man shall leave his father and mother and be
joined to his wife, and the two shall become one flesh."* ³²*This mystery is
a profound one, and I am saying that it refers to Christ and the church;*
³³*however, let each one of you love his wife as himself, and let the wife see
that she respects her husband.**

6:1 Children, obey your parents in the Lord, for this is right. ²*"Honor
your father and mother" (this is the first commandment with a promise),*
³*"that it may be well with you and that you may live long on the earth."*
⁴*Fathers, do not provoke your children to anger, but bring them up in the
discipline and instruction of the Lord.* ⁵*Slaves, be obedient to those who
are your earthly masters, with fear and trembling, in singleness of heart,
as to Christ;* ⁶*not in the way of eye-service, as men-pleasers, but as*

servants of Christ, doing the will of God from the heart, [7]rendering service with a good will as to the Lord and not to men, [8]knowing that whatever good any one does, he will receive the same again from the Lord, whether he is a slave or free. [9]Masters, do the same to them, and forbear threatening, knowing that he who is both their Master and yours is in heaven, and that there is no partiality with him.

Let me point out that RSV is at its worst in the translation of Ephesians 5:21: "Be subject to one another out of reverence for Christ." On the one hand, possibly out of excessive concern for "political correctness," it renders *phobō* as "reverence." Elsewhere RSV systematically renders *phobō* as "fear," thus preserving its original meaning. Further, RSV translates *hypotassomenoi* as "be subject." Nevertheless, if one keeps in mind the original understanding of the Latin verb *subjicio*, the source of the passive participle English "subject" and whose literal meaning is "throw (and thus place, put) under (below)," then one ends with the connotation of the original Greek verb *hypotassō* which is "subordain." *tassō* technically means "put in order" whence we have *taxis* (order) and *syntaxis* (syntax, the co-ordering of words in a sentence). An interesting passage that sheds light on this matter is the following:

If any speak in a tongue, let there be only two or at most three, and each in turn; and let one interpret. But if there is no one to interpret, let each of them keep silence in church and speak to himself and to God. Let two or three prophets speak, and let the others weigh what is said. If a revelation is made to another sitting by, let the first be silent. For you can all prophesy one by one, so that all may learn and all be encouraged; and the spirits of prophets are subject (*hypotassetai*) to prophets. For God is not a God of confusion (the opposite of "order") but of peace. As in all the churches of the saints, the women should keep silence in the churches. For they are not permitted to speak, but should be subordinate (*hypotassesthōsan*),[5] as even the law says. If there is anything they desire to know, let them ask their husbands at home. For it is shameful for a woman to speak in church. What! Did the word of God originate with you,

---

[5] Notice how RSV uses "subordinate" (sub-ordained), which is close to the original.

or are you the only ones it has reached? If any one thinks that he is a prophet, or spiritual, he should acknowledge that what I am writing to you is a command of the Lord. If any one does not recognize this, he is not recognized. So, my brethren, earnestly desire to prophesy, and do not forbid speaking in tongues; but all things should be done decently and in order (*kata taxin*; according to order; orderly). (1Cor 14:27-40)[6]

The importance of the matter lies in that both passages are dealing with "order" in the setting of a *kat' oikon ekklēsia*. Consequently, it becomes of the essence that the members of the *kat' oikon ekklēsia* are to be "subordinate *to one another (each one to the other)*" (5:21) under the aegis of Christ who alone is the Lord of the household. This explains why the one who would be hit the hardest is the *paterfamilias*, the "lord of the household," in that he will be required to "give himself (in sacrifice)" for and to "cleanse and wash" (Eph 5:26) his household. These are both actions of a house slave—the one who a few verses earlier was required to be subordinate to the *paterfamilias* (v.22). The solution to this conundrum is to be found in that the action of either is to be done in view of the fact that Christ is the Lord:

> Wives, be subject to your husbands, *as to the Lord*. For the husband is the head of the wife *as Christ* is the head of the church, his body, and is himself its Savior. As the church is subject *to Christ*, so let wives also be subject in everything to their husbands. Husbands, love your wives, *as Christ* loved the church and gave himself up for her … For no man ever hates his own flesh, but nourishes and cherishes it, *as Christ* does the church … This mystery is a profound one, and I am saying that it refers *to Christ* and the church; however, let each one of you love his wife as himself, and let the wife see that she respects[7] (*phobēsai*; fear, treats with fear) her husband. (vv.22-25, 29, 32-33)

The original wording of 5:21-6:9 is very important since it presents household rules meant to maintain order and to secure

---

[6] See my comments on this passage in *C-1Cor* 251-8.

[7] Here again RSV distorts the original.

the setting of the Pauline *kat' oikon ekklēsia*. The epistle reading of these verses during the sacrament of matrimony—at least according to the Orthodox church's rubics—makes it sound as though v. 21 pertains solely to the paterfamilias and his wife.[8] In reality the entire passage pertains to the governing of the entire Roman household—whether that of a paterfamilias or materfamilias[9]—that has fully submitted to the Lord as its *autocratic* "head." In fact, Paul unequivocally states that the "mystery" he is talking about in these verses is the "mystery" with which the entire epistle is dealing, and thus it pertains to the Christ of Ephesians and his *kat 'oikon ekklēsia*. In the "scripturalized" story of the beginnings of the "church/es," the Book of Acts purports that the first such household head is in fact a materfamilias by the name of Lydia. She trusted in Paul's teaching and, in submission to that teaching, *imposed* on *her* household her decision to make of it "the house(hold) of God (*oikō Theou*), which is the church of the living God (*ekklēsia theou zōntos*)" (1 Tim 3:15) whose new "head" is the Christ preached by Paul:

> and on the sabbath day we went outside the gate to the riverside, where we supposed there was a place of prayer; and we sat down and spoke to the women who had come together. One who heard us was a woman named Lydia, from the city of Thyatira, a seller of purple goods, who was a worshiper of God. The Lord opened her heart to give heed to what was said by Paul. And when she was baptized, *with her household*, she besought us, saying, "If you have judged me to be faithful (*pistēn*)[10] to the Lord, come to my house and stay." And she prevailed upon us. (Acts 16:13-15)

The most common scenario, however, is that of a paterfamilias rather than a materfamilias. This is evidenced in Ephesians 6:4

---

[8] The Christian tradition does the same with the Book of Song of Songs making out of it a Hallmark Card love story between God and Israel (or Jerusalem) when in reality—as part of the *ketubim*—it deals with the integration of the nations into Zion, God's city. See my comments in *OTI₃* 104-1.

[9] The oneness of this passage is evident in that the following section is introduced with *Tou loipou* (Finally; 6:10).

[10] The grammatically feminine of *pistos* that is one the classic New Testament terms referring to a believer as is the case in Eph 1:1.

where both parents (the parents), when addressed, are called *hoi pateres*, literally "the fathers". This matter of fact was even respected by the Vulgate that has *patres* (fathers), although it had the choice of using *parentes*, which is found just a few verses earlier: "Children, obey your parents (Greek *goneusin*, progenitors; Latin *parentibus*) in the Lord, for this is right." (v.1) This is the more striking when one considers that the shift from "parents" (v.1) to "fathers" (v.4) is done although the scriptural quotations in the intervening vv. 2-3 (Ex 20:12; Deut 5:16) refer to the child's "father" *and* "mother" separately.[11] Thus, the original authors could have used *hoi goneis* in Ephesians 6:4; however, they opted[12] to respect and reflect the Roman tradition.

The centrality of the paterfamilias in the entire matter of the house rules is evident in that he is part of every summons in conjunction with every other member of the *familia*:

1. The wives are addressed in relation to their husbands and not with any other household member (5:21-33).

2. The children are addressed as to their behavior toward their "parents" who, in their turn, are spoken of as "fathers" (6:1-4).

3. The required comportment of the slaves (vv.4-8) is specifically in conjunction with their *kyrioi*

---

[11] In this regard one should tip one's hat to RSV that kept close to the original: "parents" in v.1 and "fathers" in v.4. Such must have meant a great deal of restraint on the part of the RSV translation committee in view of the fact that the same RSV takes its unwarranted liberty in translating the original *zera'* (seed) in Gen 4:25 into "child" against all other translations including its parent the KJV! Perhaps, given both the close proximity of Eph 6:1 and 4 and their being within the same topic, disregard of the original would have looked too flagrant.

[12] Politically correctly, I may add as a pun.

(lords, masters; v.4), which is the plural of the
masculine *kyrios*.

4. The same *kyrioi* is found in the address to the
heads of the households (v.9).

Notice that the "liberation" of the slaves is not in Paul's purview.
This would have been a practical impossibility in the Roman
setting of the time.[13] The reason is twofold. First of all, the Lord
himself suffered the death of a slave (Phil 2:7-8); moreover, Paul,
although Roman citizen (Acts 16:37-38; 22:25-29; 23:27), viewed
himself as the slave of that same Christ (Phil 1:1). Secondly—and
this is the more practical and thus pertinent reason—slaves in the
Roman empire could not possibly become free citizens even when
granted their freedom: in such a case the status of the liberated
doulos (slave) is that of *apelevtheros* (freedman) and not *elevtheros*
(free). That is why Paul asked of his followers to remain in the
state in which each one was when "called" by God:

> Only, let every one lead the life which the Lord has assigned to him,
> and in which God has called him. This is my rule in all the churches.
> Was any one at the time of his call already circumcised? Let him not
> seek to remove the marks of circumcision. Was any one at the time
> of his call uncircumcised? Let him not seek circumcision. For
> neither circumcision counts for anything nor uncircumcision, but
> keeping the commandments of God. Every one should remain in
> the state in which he was called. Were you a slave when called?
> Never mind. But if you can gain your freedom, avail yourself of the
> opportunity. For he who was called in the Lord as a slave is a
> freedman (*apelevtheros*) of the Lord. Likewise he who was free when
> called is a slave of Christ. You were bought with a price; do not
> become slaves of men. So, brethren, in whatever state each was
> called, there let him remain with God. (1 Cor 7:17-24)[14]

---

[13] A most telling point in case is the rebellion of the Macedonian slave Spartacus.

[14] It is worth noting that this passage seems to be an aside in a chapter dealing with
marriage.

Here, in Ephesians, Paul asks the household slaves to be the "slaves of Christ"—they are no better than Paul—in doing "the will of God" while "serving" (*doulevontes*; from the verb *doulevō* [from the same root as *doulos*]) their masters "in the Lord" (6:6-7). Indirectly, he is already preparing for his address to the house lords (v.9), namely, that they and their slaves are actually serving the same Lord *as slaves*. Indeed, the so-called "lords" are themselves under the authority of the one Lord in heaven whose slaves they are *together with their own slaves*: "knowing that he who is *both their Master and yours* is in heaven, and that there is no partiality with him." (v.9) Thus, and most importantly as well as unexpectedly, a Roman paterfamilias is "not to threaten his slaves" (v.9). Rather he is to leave the matter for the impartial judge of all (v.9).

Chapter 6

Vv. 10-24 *¹⁰Τοῦ λοιποῦ ἐνδυναμοῦσθε ἐν κυρίῳ καὶ ἐν τῷ κράτει τῆς ἰσχύος αὐτοῦ ¹¹ἐνδύσασθε τὴν πανοπλίαν τοῦ θεοῦ πρὸς τὸ δύνασθαι ὑμᾶς στῆναι πρὸς τὰς μεθοδείας τοῦ διαβόλου· ¹²ὅτι οὐκ ἔστιν ἡμῖν ἡ πάλη πρὸς αἷμα καὶ σάρκα ἀλλὰ πρὸς τὰς ἀρχάς πρὸς τὰς ἐξουσίας πρὸς τοὺς κοσμοκράτορας τοῦ σκότους τούτου πρὸς τὰ πνευματικὰ τῆς πονηρίας ἐν τοῖς ἐπουρανίοις ¹³διὰ τοῦτο ἀναλάβετε τὴν πανοπλίαν τοῦ θεοῦ ἵνα δυνηθῆτε ἀντιστῆναι ἐν τῇ ἡμέρᾳ τῇ πονηρᾷ καὶ ἅπαντα κατεργασάμενοι στῆναι ¹⁴στῆτε οὖν περιζωσάμενοι τὴν ὀσφὺν ὑμῶν ἐν ἀληθείᾳ καὶ ἐνδυσάμενοι τὸν θώρακα τῆς δικαιοσύνης ¹⁵καὶ ὑποδησάμενοι τοὺς πόδας ἐν ἑτοιμασίᾳ τοῦ εὐαγγελίου τῆς εἰρήνης· ¹⁶ἐν πᾶσιν ἀναλαβόντες τὸν θυρεὸν τῆς πίστεως ἐν ᾧ δυνήσεσθε πάντα τὰ βέλη τοῦ πονηροῦ τὰ πεπυρωμένα σβέσαι· ¹⁷καὶ τὴν περικεφαλαίαν τοῦ σωτηρίου δέξασθε καὶ τὴν μάχαιραν τοῦ πνεύματος ὅ ἐστιν ῥῆμα θεοῦ ¹⁸Διὰ πάσης προσευχῆς καὶ δεήσεως προσευχόμενοι ἐν παντὶ καιρῷ ἐν πνεύματί καὶ εἰς αὐτὸ ἀγρυπνοῦντες ἐν πάσῃ προσκαρτερήσει καὶ δεήσει περὶ πάντων τῶν ἁγίων ¹⁹καὶ ὑπὲρ ἐμοῦ ἵνα μοι δοθῇ λόγος ἐν ἀνοίξει τοῦ στόματός μού ἐν παρρησίᾳ γνωρίσαι τὸ μυστήριον τοῦ εὐαγγελίου ²⁰ὑπὲρ οὗ πρεσβεύω ἐν ἁλύσεί ἵνα ἐν αὐτῷ παρρησιάσωμαι ὡς δεῖ με λαλῆσαί ²¹Ἵνα δὲ εἰδῆτε καὶ ὑμεῖς τὰ κατ᾽ ἐμέ τί πράσσω πάντα γνωρίσει ὑμῖν Τύχικος ὁ ἀγαπητὸς ἀδελφὸς καὶ πιστὸς διάκονος ἐν κυρίῳ ²²ὃν ἔπεμψα πρὸς ὑμᾶς εἰς αὐτὸ τοῦτό ἵνα γνῶτε τὰ περὶ ἡμῶν καὶ παρακαλέσῃ τὰς καρδίας ὑμῶν ²³Εἰρήνη τοῖς ἀδελφοῖς καὶ ἀγάπη μετὰ πίστεως ἀπὸ θεοῦ πατρὸς καὶ κυρίου Ἰησοῦ Χριστοῦ ²⁴ἡ χάρις μετὰ πάντων τῶν ἀγαπώντων τὸν κύριον ἡμῶν Ἰησοῦν Χριστὸν ἐν ἀφθαρσίᾳ*

¹⁰Finally, be strong in the Lord and in the strength of his might.¹¹Put on the whole armor of God, that you may be able to stand against the wiles of the devil. [12]For we are not contending against flesh and blood, but against the principalities, against the powers, against the world rulers of this present darkness, against the spiritual hosts of wickedness in the heavenly places. [13]Therefore take the whole armor of God, that you may be able to withstand in the evil day, and having done all, to stand. [14]Stand therefore, having girded your loins with truth, and having put on the breastplate of righteousness, [15]and having shod your feet with the equipment of the gospel of peace; [16]besides all these, taking the shield of faith, with which you can quench all the flaming darts of the evil one. [17]And take the helmet of salvation, and the sword of the Spirit, which is the word of God. [18]Pray at all times in the Spirit, with all prayer and supplication. To that end keep alert with all perseverance, making supplication for all the saints, [19]and also for me, that utterance may be given me in opening my mouth boldly to proclaim the mystery of the gospel, [20]for which I am an ambassador in chains; that I may declare it boldly, as I ought to speak [21]Now that you also may know how I am and what I am doing, Tychicus the beloved brother and faithful minister in the Lord will tell you everything. [22]I have sent him to you for this very purpose, that you may know how we are, and that he may encourage your hearts. [23]Peace be to the brethren, and love with faith, from God the Father and the Lord Jesus Christ. [24]Grace be with all who love our Lord Jesus Christ with love undying.

In five and a half chapters, Paul has firmly established in the minds of his hearers that their new everyday reality lies in neither an imaginary outlandish heaven à la Plato, nor in an imaginary "mysterious" universal "church," à la later theology. Rather this new reality lies in the immediate daily context of their own Roman household. Within the confines of the Roman empire everyone, whoever one might be, is de facto a member of a Roman household. This statement should be taken not only literally, but also literarily, given that *all* Paul's letters are addressed to churches or individuals living within those confines. Add to this that, depending on the addressees, each of the letters reflects and deals with some of the traits of the city they live in. For example, it is no coincidence that the letter to the Romans revolves around (imperial) "power" and (legal) "righteousness," and that to the Corinthians puts down (Greek) human "wisdom." So unless we make the effort to perceive the message of each letter with the ears of its original addressees, we are bound to misunderstand its message by "universalizing" it "philosophically" or "theologically."[1] Still, what binds together the entire Pauline corpus and, by extension, the entire New Testament is the setting of the first century A.D. Roman empire whose social backbone or fabric is the Roman *domus* whose Greek counterpart is *oikos*. It is by sowing the seed of the scriptural *qahal* (Hebrew) or *ekklēsia* (Greek)—through his letter writing—in some of the Roman *oikoi* (households)[2] Paul had *hope*[3]—sometimes against or beyond (human) hope (Rom 4:18)—that the scriptural divine *sod* (Hebrew: counsel, mystery) will be unveiled to the nations of the Roman empire.

Having accomplished this mission, in the remainder of the letter Paul exhorts his hearers to proceed in perseverance on that path, since salvation still lies ahead (Eph 6:17a; see also 1 Thess 5:8b): "To that end keep alert with all perseverance." (Eph 6:18b) The process or progress while on the path is a staple of the Pauline letters, which goes hand in hand with hope, another staple in his writings:

> Therefore, since we are justified by faith, we have peace with God through our Lord Jesus Christ. Through him we have obtained access to this grace in which we stand, and we rejoice in our hope of sharing the glory of God. More than that, we rejoice in our sufferings, knowing that suffering produces endurance, and endurance produces character, and character produces hope, and hope does not disappoint us, because God's love has been poured

---

[1] Just as a resident of the lush New England filled with rivers and forests *cannot* possibly hear, let alone pray, Psalm 93 in the same way as someone cognizant of, if not living in, the Syrian Wilderness of those times.

[2] Acts 11:14; 16:15, 31; 18:8; 1 Cor 1:16; 16:15.

[3] Which is a ubiquitous term in his letters.

into our hearts through the Holy Spirit which has been given to us. (Rom 5:1-5)

You are severed from Christ, you who would be justified by the law; you have fallen away from grace. For through the Spirit, by faith, we wait for the hope of righteousness. (Gal 5:4-5)

for through him we both have access in one Spirit to the Father. So then you are no longer strangers and sojourners, but you are fellow citizens with the saints and members of the household of God, built upon the foundation of the apostles and prophets, Christ Jesus himself being the cornerstone, in whom the whole structure is joined together and grows into a holy temple in the Lord; in whom you also are built into it for a dwelling place of God in the Spirit. (Eph 2:18-22)

And I am sure that he who began a good work in you will bring it to completion at the day of Jesus Christ. (Phil 1:6)

We give thanks to God always for you all, constantly mentioning you in our prayers, remembering before our God and Father your work of faith and labor of love and steadfastness of hope in our Lord Jesus Christ. (1Thess 1:2-3)

However, the path is not an easy one since the enemies are mighty (principalities, powers, world rulers of this present darkness, spiritual hosts of wickedness in the heavenly places; Eph 6:12) and will use any weapon in their possession (the wiles of the devil [v.11] and all the flaming darts of the evil one [v.16]) to block the advance of the believers toward the end. That is why the believers are asked to put on an armor that is thoroughly defensive: girdle (v.14), breastplate (v.14), sandals (v.15), shield (v.16), helmet (v.17). The only aggressive weapon is the (Roman) sword, yet this time around the sword is the Spirit's and it is tantamount to the "word of God" (v.17), the "gospel" that will bring about God's peace (v.15) instead of the *pax Romana*. Although this weaponry "sounds" weak and ineffective compared to the Roman sword, the outcome of victory, of "withstanding [the attack] in the evil day" and ultimately "standing (tall)" (v.13),

is assured since the God, whose armor the believers are asked to
don (vv.11 and 13), is none other than the one whose "strength
of his might" (v.10) was already behind the entire plan being
implemented:

> ... and what is the immeasurable greatness of his power (*dynameōs*)
> in us who believe, according to the working of his great might (*tou
> kratous tēs iskhyos avtou*). (Eph 1:19)

> Finally, be strong (*endynamousthe*) in the Lord and in the strength of
> his might (*tō kratei tēs iskhyos avtou*). (6:10)

Still, while on the path and, precisely because the end has not
yet come, the addressees are asked, while persevering, to keep
praying for all the other "saints" (6:18) and especially for Paul,
who de facto is the one carrying the mystery of the gospel in *his*
words which contain the word of God, so that he may continue
doing this until his upcoming demise, since he is "in chains"
(vv.19-20). And just in case his demise happens before the end,
he is sending their way Tychicus the "faithful (trustworthy)
minister (*diakonos*)" (v.21) who would continue Paul's ministry
(3:7) and encourage (*parakalese*) their hearts (6:22). Since the Greek
tykhē means "fate, chance, fortuity," Tychicus (*Tykhikos*) is anyone
God may choose, thus indicating that God will remain in control
of the situation after the departure of Paul, and thus the Ephesians
need not worry. In other words, Tychicus will implement Paul's
mission of *diakonia*. However, a caveat is in order here.
Theologians across all denominations misconstrue Paul's intent
by assuming that God would choose anyone who will become
another Paul, so to speak. This is how church leaders and
theologians like to view themselves, forgetting that there is only
one Paul. Were it not so, why should he have bothered writing so
extensively while not allowing his addressees to be misled or "to
be quickly shaken in mind or excited, either by spirit or by word,
or by letter purporting to be from us" (2 Thess 2:2)? His intention
was fully captured in 2 Pet 3:15-16:

Therefore, beloved, since you wait for these, be zealous to be found by him without spot or blemish, and at peace. And count the forbearance of our Lord as salvation. So also our beloved brother Paul wrote to you according to the wisdom given him, speaking of this as he does in all his letters. There are some things in them hard to understand, which the ignorant and unstable twist to their own destruction, as they do the other scriptures.

Since the New Testament Paul is a scripturalized Paul, so are all his adjutants. Consequently, Tychicus is meant to be anyone who would continue Paul's teaching through repeating the scripturalized words of the Apostle to the hearing of the members of the *kat' oikon ekklesiai* (household churches), in the same way as Jeremiah and Ezekiel did with God's "words." This understanding finds confirmation in the New Testament itself. The reference to Tychicus at the end of Ephesians is found again virtually *verbatim* toward the end of Colossians, the companion letter:

Now that you also may know how I am and what I am doing, Tychicus the beloved brother and faithful minister in the Lord will tell you everything. I have sent him to you for this very purpose, that you may know how we are, and that he may encourage your hearts. (Eph 6:21-22)

Tychicus will tell you all about my affairs; he is a beloved brother and faithful minister and fellow servant in the Lord. I have sent him to you for this very purpose, that you may know how we are and that he may encourage your hearts. (Col 4:7-8)

Such cannot possibly be happenstance. It is as though the hearer is invited to understand the Ephesians text in the light of that in Colossians. The text regarding Tychicus in Ephesians appears just before the final greeting (vv.23-24), whereas in Colossians the same text is followed by nine other verses (vv.9-17) before the final greeting in v.18.[4] This being the case, then the mention of

---

[4] I refer my readers to my Commentary on Colossians where I explain that the ending of Colossians (4:7-18) functions as a coverage of the New Testament canon of books. *C-Col* 95-106.

Tychicus at this point (v.7-8) in Colossians is a literary device meant to introduce him as being any reader who would point to or, better, recite to the members of any *kat' oikon ekklesia* the actual content of the New Testament starting with the Pauline corpus, just as the *anaginōskōn* (the one reading aloud) "the words of the prophecy" (Rev 1:3) does. This, in turn, explains the otherwise enigmatic "let the reader (*anaginōskōn*) understand" (Mat 24:15//Mk 13:14).[5]

Paul usually ends his letters by wishing (God's) grace upon his hearers (Gal 6:18; Phil 4:23; Col 4:18; 1 Thess 5:28; 1 Thess 3:18; 1 Tim 6:21; 2 Tim 4:22; Tit 3:15; Philem 25; Heb 13:25); however, one notices three exceptions, which also mention "love":

> If any one has no love for the Lord, let him be accursed. Our Lord, come! The grace of the Lord Jesus be with you. My love be with you all in Christ Jesus. Amen. (1 Cor 16:22-24)

> The grace of the Lord Jesus Christ and the love of God and the fellowship of the Holy Spirit be with you all. (2 Cor 13:14)

> Peace be to the brethren, and love with faith, from God the Father and the Lord Jesus Christ. Grace be with all who love our Lord Jesus Christ with love undying (*en aphtharsia*). (Eph 6:23-24)

The two-verse ending of Ephesians is definitely a stunning tour de force. It combines in a very compact form the four major terms—peace, love, faith, and grace—that do not appear in their totality at the end of any of the other letters:

> *Peace* be to the brethren, and *love* (*agapē*) with *faith* (*pisteōs*), from God the Father and the Lord Jesus Christ. *Grace* (*kharis*) be with all who

---

[5] I am still astonished at how many Protestant exegetes, programmed by their own tradition, explain this aside as addressed to all of us, i.e., each and every one of us, who are "reading" scripture for ourselves. Notice how RSV added "aloud" after "the one who reads" (Rev 1:3) only because it was forced by the following "those (in the plural case) who hear (*hoi akouontes*)," whereas it omits it in Mt and Mk. However, in the original Greek, we have the same *anaginōskōn* (singular case) in all three passages.

love (*agapōntōn*) our Lord Jesus Christ with *love undying*[6] (*en aphtharsia*; in (unto) incorruption [incorruptibility]). (6:23-24)

This ending is a befitting close of a bracket stretching over the entire epistle that started in the opening few verses:

> Paul, an apostle of Christ Jesus by the will of God, To the saints who are also faithful (*pistois*) in Christ Jesus: *Grace* to you and *peace* from God our Father and the Lord Jesus Christ. Blessed be the God and Father of our Lord Jesus Christ, who has blessed us in Christ with every spiritual blessing in the heavenly places, even as he chose us in him before the foundation of the world, that we should be holy and blameless before him. He destined us in *love* to be his sons through Jesus Christ, according to the purpose of his will, to the praise of his glorious *grace* which he freely bestowed on us in the *Beloved* (*ēgapēmenō*). In him we have redemption through his blood, the forgiveness of our trespasses, according to the riches of his *grace* which he lavished upon us. For he has made known to us in all wisdom and insight *the mystery of his will*, according to his purpose which he set forth in Christ as a plan for the fulness of time, to unite all things in him, things in heaven and things on earth. In him, according to the purpose of him who accomplishes all things according to the counsel of his will, we who first hoped in Christ have been destined and appointed to live for the praise of his glory. In him you also, who have heard the word of truth, the gospel of your salvation, and *have believed* (*pistevsantes*) in him, were sealed with the promised Holy Spirit, which is the guarantee of our inheritance until we acquire possession of it, to the praise of his glory. For this reason, because I have heard of your *faith* in the Lord Jesus and your *love* toward all the saint. (1:1-15)

Thus the author is locking his addressees "on the way" toward the realization of God's "mystery" which he "willed" (v.9) for them through a "plan" (*oikonomia*) he devised for that purpose, *hē oikonomia tou mystēriou* (3:9). The plan was revealed to Paul who, in turn, consigned it fully in this letter both materially and formally:

---

[6] A loose translation of the original found only in RSV.

To me, though I am the very least of all the saints, this grace was given, to preach to the Gentiles the unsearchable riches of Christ, and to make all men see what is the plan of the mystery hidden for ages in God who created all things; that through the (house) church (in Ephesus) the manifold wisdom of God might now be made known to the principalities and powers in the heavenly places. (3:8-10)

That is why the Ephesians are asked to submit to the teaching scripturalized in this letter *until the end*, that is, until they attain the heavenly places where their already glorified Lord is waiting for them: "Blessed be the God and Father of our Lord Jesus Christ, who has blessed us in Christ with every spiritual blessing in the heavenly places." (1:3) This is precisely what is intended and meant with the enigmatic final phrase *en aphtharsia* (in [unto] incorruption, incorruptibility, imperishability) (6:24).[7] In fact, the hearer of the Pauline corpus in its canonical setting has no other choice considering that the preceding occurrences of that noun, without exception, point to the future life in the glory of the resurrected:

Claiming to be wise, they became fools, and exchanged the glory of the immortal (*aphtharton*; incorruptible, imperishable)[8] God for images resembling mortal (*phartou*; corruptible, perishable)[9] man or birds or animals or reptiles. (Rom 1:22-23)

For he will render to every man according to his works: to those who by patience in well-doing seek for glory and honor and immortality (*aphtharsian*; incorruption, incorruptibility, imperishability),[10] he will give eternal life; but for those who are

---

[7] See Vulgate (*in incorruptione*), JB (*dans la vie incorruptible*), Arabic AVD (*fi 'adami-lphasad* [in incorruption]). KJV and RSV are obviously at a loss and render it either "in sincerity" (KJV) or "with love undying," both obviously missing the point.

[8] Vulgate has *incorruptibilis*.

[9] Vulgate has *corruptibilis*.

[10] Vulgate has *incorruptionem*.

factious and do not obey the truth, but obey wickedness, there will be wrath and fury. (2:6-8)

Every athlete exercises self-control in all things. They do it to receive a perishable (*phtharton*)[11] wreath, but we an imperishable (*aphtharton*).[12] (1 Cor 9:25)

So is it with the resurrection of the dead. What is sown is perishable (*en phthora*; in, unto corruption), what is raised is imperishable (*en aphtharsia*).[13] It is sown in dishonor, it is raised in glory. It is sown in weakness, it is raised in power. It is sown a physical body, it is raised a spiritual body. If there is a physical body, there is also a spiritual body. (15:42-44)

I tell you this, brethren: flesh and blood cannot inherit the kingdom of God, nor does the perishable (*hē phthora*; the corruption, perishability) inherit the imperishable (*tēn aphtharsian*; the incorruption, corruptibility, perishability). Lo! I tell you a mystery. We shall not all sleep, but we shall all be changed, in a moment, in the twinkling of an eye, at the last trumpet. For the trumpet will sound, and the dead will be raised imperishable (*aphthartoi*), and we shall be changed. For this perishable nature (*to phtharton touto*) must put on the imperishable (*aphtharsian*), and this mortal nature must put on immortality. When the perishable (*to phtharton*) puts on the imperishable, and the mortal puts on immortality, then shall come to pass the saying that is written: "Death is swallowed up in victory." (vv.50-54)

---

[11] Vulgate has *corruptibilem*.

[12] Vulgate has *incorruptam*.

[13] Which is exactly the same phrase found in Eph 6:24.

2 Thessalonians

Introduction

Throughout my entire corpus of work I have repeatedly and in various ways indicated and shown that since the scriptural writings were conceived to be heard, their total as well as the individual structure of each book is essentially repetitive, aimed at drilling the message into the ears and, hopefully, the minds of the hearers. However, the repetitiveness does not translate in a series of copycat writings. Rather, each unit—whether a book or letter or part thereof—is ingeniously written for a specific group of hearers posited in different settings and circumstances. Let me give a few examples in an illustrative manner.

- Exodus and Deuteronomy that deal with the delivery of the divine statutes are set at two different times and in two different circumstances separated by a long trek of forty years through the wilderness. Moreover, the former is addressed to people who were just brought *out of* Egypt whereas in the latter the people are about to be brought *into* the earth of Canaan.

- The Books of Samuel and Kings, on the one hand, and the Books of Chronicles, on the other hand, basically cover the Kingdoms of Judah and Israel until the fall of Jerusalem. Samuel and Kings are part of the *nebi'im* (Prophets), which is the second part of the Old Testament; Chronicles is relegated to the end of the *ketubim* (Writings), which is the third part of the Old Testament. Moreover, in the Hebrew canon, the Books of Chronicles *follow* Ezra and Nehemiah that cover the *later* period of the return from the Babylonian exile.

- The basic message of the Latter Prophets (Isaiah, Jeremiah, Ezekiel, and the Scroll of the Twelve) is essentially the same, and thus sounds boringly repetitive to both an inveterate and a first-time hearer of scripture. Yet the time setting of each Book is different. Structure wise, the books of the Latter Prophets are conceived as an inversion (A-B-B'-A'), whereby the first, Isaiah, corresponds to the last, the Twelve, in that their content spans a long period, that is, from the establishment of Kingdoms of Israel and Judah until the return from the exile. The two central Books, Jeremiah and Ezekiel, revolve around the fall of Jerusalem, the one set in Judah and the other in Babylon.

- Two good examples of "repetitions" within the same book are found in Genesis and Ezekiel. In Genesis we hear of famine in conjunction with Abraham (twice), Isaac, and Jacob. The first instance with Abraham/Abram brings him into bondage under Pharaoh in Egypt ("Now there was a famine in the land. So Abram went down to Egypt to sojourn there, for the famine was severe in the land" Gen 12:10). This looks ahead to the similar predicament—and for the same reason of famine ("So ten of Joseph's brothers went down to buy grain in Egypt …Thus the sons of Israel came to buy among the others who came, for the famine was in the land of Canaan;" Gen 42:3, 5)— that befell Jacob and his progeny. In the case of Isaac the reference to "a famine in the land, besides the former famine that was in the days of Abraham" (Gen 26:1) prepares for the introduction of another parallelism between the two patriarchs: the encounter with the Philistines (Abraham in Gen 21:22-34 and Isaac in Gen 26:7-35). The intentionality of the link is sealed in that Isaac incurs with Abimelech the Philistine the same kind of predicament Abram/Abraham encountered with both Pharaoh and Abimelech concerning their wives, and the lie they both had to come up with to present their wives as being their sisters.

- In Ezekiel, one hears thrice of the harlotry of the people in Canaan (chs.16, 20, 23). Yet despite the fact that 16 and 23 are essentially similar, in the former we repeatedly hear (six times) of Sodom, as third sister to Samaria and Jerusalem, with no mention at all of her in the latter.

- In the New Testament we have four Gospel Books with numerous repetitions. Luke is divided into two "words" (Acts 1:1): the Gospel of Luke and the Book of Acts, the latter forming the link to Paul's apostolic activity in a story form and also functioning as an introduction to Paul's written legacy.

In all my commentaries on Paul's letters I have stressed that his written legacy was intentionally aimed at different cities covering the entire expanse of the Roman empire so that the hearer, at the end of the day, would get the distinct impression that Paul is indeed *the* Apostle to all the different nations residing within that empire. Furthermore, the message of each of his letters is tailored, vocabulary and phraseology wise, to correspond to the actual addressees in their setting within the Roman empire. The result is that the repetitiveness is conceived along the lines of the opening of the Epistle to the Hebrews that captured the heart of this intentional literary device of scripture: "In many and various ways God spoke of old to our fathers by the prophets" (Heb 1:1 RSV); "God, who at sundry times (*polymerōs*) and in divers manners (*polytropōs*) spake in time past unto the fathers by the prophets." (Heb 1:1 KJV) So also Paul wrote "in many and various ways" to the different churches expounding the *one* gospel of God whose *one* apostle to the Gentiles he was, to extent that he could refer to the gospel as being equally "his": "my gospel" (Rom 2:16; 16:25; 2 Tim 2:8); "our gospel" (2 Cor 4:3; 2 Thess 2:14). This apparent extremism makes sense in view of his statement in Galatians:

> But when he who had set me apart before I was born, and had called me through his grace, was pleased to reveal his Son to me *(en emoi)*, in order that I might preach him among the Gentiles, I did not confer with flesh and blood ... And they glorified God *because of me (en emoi)*. (Gal 1:15-16, 24 RSV)

> But when it pleased God, who separated me from my mother's womb, and called *me* by his grace, To reveal his Son *in me (en emoi)*, that I might preach him among the heathen; immediately I conferred not with flesh and blood ... And they glorified God *in me (en emoi)*. (Gal 1: 15-16, 24 KJV)

Given all the preceding it stands to reason that the Thessalonian correspondence plays a double role. On the one hand, it is addressed to the capital of Macedonia, the land of Alexander whose feats triggered the rise of scripture and, as such, wraps up the entire Pauline corpus of epistles addressed to churches. Even the setup of that correspondence is magisterial. The first letter sets the tone for the second in that the latter assumes that the message of 1 Thessalonians 4:13-5:11 concerning the Lord's coming was not heeded. So 2 Thessalonians repeats this warning in three different versions following the scriptural device of warning not once, not twice, but three times. And since it is the gospel message that forewarns the Gentiles of the forthcoming judgement of all (Rom 2:16), it is understandable that the triple message of 2 Thessalonians revolves around that gospel. This further explains why it is cast in a vocabulary reminiscent of the previous Pauline epistles. So in order not to burden my readers with material they could readily find in my previous commentaries and studies, I shall approach this letter (1) by simply indicating the similarities between its content and that of the preceding epistles and (2) by pointing out in which sense the gospel preached by Paul not only forewarns of the Lord's coming, but also "produces" or at least "triggers" it.[1] The second concern is, in a way, the trademark of 2 Thessalonians.

---

[1] See Excursus 1.

Chapter 1

Vv. 1-12 ¹Παῦλος καὶ Σιλουανὸς καὶ Τιμόθεος τῇ ἐκκλησίᾳ Θεσσαλονικέων ἐν θεῷ πατρὶ ἡμῶν καὶ κυρίῳ Ἰησοῦ Χριστῷ· ²χάρις ὑμῖν καὶ εἰρήνη ἀπὸ θεοῦ πατρὸς ἡμῶν καὶ κυρίου Ἰησοῦ Χριστοῦ ³Εὐχαριστεῖν ὀφείλομεν τῷ θεῷ πάντοτε περὶ ὑμῶν ἀδελφοί καθὼς ἄξιόν ἐστιν ὅτι ὑπεραυξάνει ἡ πίστις ὑμῶν καὶ πλεονάζει ἡ ἀγάπη ἑνὸς ἑκάστου πάντων ὑμῶν εἰς ἀλλήλους ⁴ὥστε αὐτοὺς ἡμᾶς ἐν ὑμῖν ἐγκαυχᾶσθαι ἐν ταῖς ἐκκλησίαις τοῦ θεοῦ ὑπὲρ τῆς ὑπομονῆς ὑμῶν καὶ πίστεως ἐν πᾶσιν τοῖς διωγμοῖς ὑμῶν καὶ ταῖς θλίψεσιν αἷς ἀνέχεσθέ ⁵ἔνδειγμα τῆς δικαίας κρίσεως τοῦ θεοῦ εἰς τὸ καταξιωθῆναι ὑμᾶς τῆς βασιλείας τοῦ θεοῦ ὑπὲρ ἧς καὶ πάσχετέ ⁶εἴπερ δίκαιον παρὰ θεῷ ἀνταποδοῦναι τοῖς θλίβουσιν ὑμᾶς θλῖψιν ⁷καὶ ὑμῖν τοῖς θλιβομένοις ἄνεσιν μεθ᾽ ἡμῶν ἐν τῇ ἀποκαλύψει τοῦ κυρίου Ἰησοῦ ἀπ᾽ οὐρανοῦ μετ᾽ ἀγγέλων δυνάμεως αὐτοῦ ⁸ἐν πυρὶ φλογός διδόντος ἐκδίκησιν τοῖς μὴ εἰδόσιν θεὸν καὶ τοῖς μὴ ὑπακούουσιν τῷ εὐαγγελίῳ τοῦ κυρίου ἡμῶν Ἰησοῦ ⁹οἵτινες δίκην τίσουσιν ὄλεθρον αἰώνιον ἀπὸ προσώπου τοῦ κυρίου καὶ ἀπὸ τῆς δόξης τῆς ἰσχύος αὐτοῦ ¹⁰ὅταν ἔλθῃ ἐνδοξασθῆναι ἐν τοῖς ἁγίοις αὐτοῦ καὶ θαυμασθῆναι ἐν πᾶσιν τοῖς πιστεύσασιν ὅτι ἐπιστεύθη τὸ μαρτύριον ἡμῶν ἐφ᾽ ὑμᾶς ἐν τῇ ἡμέρᾳ ἐκείνῃ ¹¹Εἰς ὃ καὶ προσευχόμεθα πάντοτε περὶ ὑμῶν ἵνα ὑμᾶς ἀξιώσῃ τῆς κλήσεως ὁ θεὸς ἡμῶν καὶ πληρώσῃ πᾶσαν εὐδοκίαν ἀγαθωσύνης καὶ ἔργον πίστεως ἐν δυνάμει ¹²ὅπως ἐνδοξασθῇ τὸ ὄνομα τοῦ κυρίου ἡμῶν Ἰησοῦ ἐν ὑμῖν καὶ ὑμεῖς ἐν αὐτῷ κατὰ τὴν χάριν τοῦ θεοῦ ἡμῶν καὶ κυρίου Ἰησοῦ Χριστοῦ

¹Paul, Silvanus, and Timothy, To the church of the Thessalonians in God our Father and the Lord Jesus Christ: ²Grace to you and peace from God the Father and the Lord Jesus Christ. ³We are bound to give thanks to God always for you, brethren, as is fitting, because your faith

121

is growing abundantly, and the love of every one of you for one another is increasing. [4]Therefore we ourselves boast of you in the churches of God for your steadfastness and faith in all your persecutions and in the afflictions which you are enduring. [5]This is evidence of the righteous judgment of God, that you may be made worthy of the kingdom of God, for which you are suffering—[6]since indeed God deems it just to repay with affliction those who afflict you, [7]and to grant rest with us to you who are afflicted, when the Lord Jesus is revealed from heaven with his mighty angels in flaming fire, [8]inflicting vengeance upon those who do not know God and upon those who do not obey the gospel of our Lord Jesus. [9]They shall suffer the punishment of eternal destruction and exclusion from the presence of the Lord and from the glory of his might, [10]when he comes on that day to be glorified in his saints, and to be marveled at in all who have believed, because our testimony to you was believed. [11]To this end we always pray for you, that our God may make you worthy of his call, and may fulfil every good resolve and work of faith by his power, [12]so that the name of our Lord Jesus may be glorified in you, and you in him, according to the grace of our God and the Lord Jesus Christ.

After the traditional greeting of wishing God's grace and peace on his addressees,[1] Paul offers in their behalf, as a high priest would, thanksgiving to God for maintaining them on the way of trust (faith) expressed in love with the steadfastness required by their hope (1 Thess 1:3)[2] in spite of the difficulties strewn by the opponent (2 Thess 2:4) in the form of persecutions and afflictions[3] which the believers, nevertheless, have to endure without exacting their own revenge.[4] The sole avenger is God himself who will intervene in his own time when he will show to everyone that he is both the just judge and is able to act accordingly. Here in 1:8 Paul introduces the opponent as those who do not know God or do not submit to the gospel concerning the Lord Jesus, a topic he will develop in the following chapter.

---

[1] As is the case in all the preceding letters.

[2] See also Rom 5:1-8; 1 Cor 13:13; Gal 5:5-6; Col 1:3-5, 21-23.

[3] Rom 5:3; 2 Cor 1:3-6; Phil 1:27-30; Col 1:24; 1 Thess 3:4.

[4] See Rom 12:16-21.

The behavior required of the Thessalonians is that they faithfully proceed on the path since God's glory and might are already present—although not fully revealed—to the believers in the power he gives them to endure the afflictions (v.11). The fullness of revelation, when they will join in glory the Lord Jesus (v.12), will take place "in its own time" (2:6). Compare the following passages in Ephesians and Colossians with the end of 2 Thessalonians 1:

> that the God of our Lord Jesus Christ, the Father of glory (*doxēs*), may give you a spirit of wisdom and of revelation in the knowledge of him, having the eyes of your hearts enlightened, that you may know what is the hope to which he has called you, what are the riches of his glorious (*tēs doxēs*) inheritance in the saints, and what is the immeasurable greatness of his power (*dynameōs*) in us who believe, according to the working (*energeian*)[5] of his great (*kratous*) might (*iskhyos*). (Eph 1:17-19)

> May you be strengthened with all power (*dynamei*), according to his glorious (*tēs doxēs*) might (*kratos*), for all endurance and patience with joy, giving thanks to the Father, who has qualified us to share in the inheritance of the saints in light. (Col 1:11-12)

> They shall suffer the punishment of eternal destruction and exclusion from the presence of the Lord and from the glory (*doxēs*) of his might (*iskhyos*), when he comes on that day to be glorified (*endoxasthēnai*) in his saints, and to be marveled at in all who have believed, because our testimony to you was believed. To this end we always pray for you, that our God may make you worthy of his call, and may fulfil every good resolve and work of faith by his power (*en dynamei*), so that the name of our Lord Jesus may be glorified (*endoxasthē*) in you, and you in him, according to the grace of our God and the Lord Jesus Christ. (2 Thess 1:9-12)

---

[5] See 2 Thess 2: "For the mystery of lawlessness is already at work (*energeitai*); only he who now restrains it will do so until he is out of the way. And then the lawless one will be revealed, and the Lord Jesus will slay him with the breath of his mouth and destroy him by his appearing and his coming. The coming of the lawless one by the activity (*energeian*) of Satan will be with all power (*dynamei*) and with pretended signs and wonders." (vv.7-9)

Chapter 2

Vv. 1-17 ¹Ἐρωτῶμεν δὲ ὑμᾶς ἀδελφοί ὑπὲρ τῆς παρουσίας τοῦ κυρίου ἡμῶν Ἰησοῦ Χριστοῦ καὶ ἡμῶν ἐπισυναγωγῆς ἐπ᾿ αὐτὸν ²εἰς τὸ μὴ ταχέως σαλευθῆναι ὑμᾶς ἀπὸ τοῦ νοὸς μηδὲ θροεῖσθαί μήτε διὰ πνεύματος μήτε διὰ λόγου μήτε δι᾿ ἐπιστολῆς ὡς δι᾿ ἡμῶν ὡς ὅτι ἐνέστηκεν ἡ ἡμέρα τοῦ κυρίου· ³Μή τις ὑμᾶς ἐξαπατήσῃ κατὰ μηδένα τρόπον ὅτι ἐὰν μὴ ἔλθῃ ἡ ἀποστασία πρῶτον καὶ ἀποκαλυφθῇ ὁ ἄνθρωπος τῆς ἀνομίας ὁ υἱὸς τῆς ἀπωλείας ⁴ὁ ἀντικείμενος καὶ ὑπεραιρόμενος ἐπὶ πάντα λεγόμενον θεὸν ἢ σέβασμα ὥστε αὐτὸν εἰς τὸν ναὸν τοῦ θεοῦ καθίσαι ἀποδεικνύντα ἑαυτὸν ὅτι ἔστιν θεός· ⁵Οὐ μνημονεύετε ὅτι ἔτι ὢν πρὸς ὑμᾶς ταῦτα ἔλεγον ὑμῖν· ⁶καὶ νῦν τὸ κατέχον οἴδατε εἰς τὸ ἀποκαλυφθῆναι αὐτὸν ἐν τῷ ἑαυτοῦ καιρῷ ⁷τὸ γὰρ μυστήριον ἤδη ἐνεργεῖται τῆς ἀνομίας· μόνον ὁ κατέχων ἄρτι ἕως ἐκ μέσου γένηται· ⁸καὶ τότε ἀποκαλυφθήσεται ὁ ἄνομος ὃν ὁ κύριος Ἰησοῦς ἀνελεῖ τῷ πνεύματι τοῦ στόματος αὐτοῦ καὶ καταργήσει τῇ ἐπιφανείᾳ τῆς παρουσίας αὐτοῦ ⁹οὗ ἐστιν ἡ παρουσία κατ᾿ ἐνέργειαν τοῦ σατανᾶ ἐν πάσῃ δυνάμει καὶ σημείοις καὶ τέρασιν ψεύδους ¹⁰καὶ ἐν πάσῃ ἀπάτῃ ἀδικίας τοῖς ἀπολλυμένοις ἀνθ᾿ ὧν τὴν ἀγάπην τῆς ἀληθείας οὐκ ἐδέξαντο εἰς τὸ σωθῆναι αὐτούς ¹¹καὶ διὰ τοῦτο πέμπει αὐτοῖς ὁ θεὸς ἐνέργειαν πλάνης εἰς τὸ πιστεῦσαι αὐτοὺς τῷ ψεύδει ¹²ἵνα κριθῶσιν πάντες οἱ μὴ πιστεύσαντες τῇ ἀληθείᾳ ἀλλὰ εὐδοκήσαντες τῇ ἀδικίᾳ ¹³ἡμεῖς δὲ ὀφείλομεν εὐχαριστεῖν τῷ θεῷ πάντοτε περὶ ὑμῶν ἀδελφοὶ ἠγαπημένοι ὑπὸ κυρίου ὅτι εἵλατο ὑμᾶς ὁ θεὸς ἀπαρχὴν εἰς σωτηρίαν ἐν ἁγιασμῷ πνεύματος καὶ πίστει ἀληθείας ¹⁴εἰς ὃ καὶ ἐκάλεσεν ὑμᾶς διὰ τοῦ εὐαγγελίου ἡμῶν εἰς περιποίησιν δόξης τοῦ κυρίου ἡμῶν Ἰησοῦ Χριστοῦ ¹⁵Ἄρα οὖν ἀδελφοί στήκετε καὶ κρατεῖτε τὰς παραδόσεις ἃς ἐδιδάχθητε εἴτε διὰ λόγου εἴτε δι᾿ ἐπιστολῆς ἡμῶν ¹⁶Αὐτὸς δὲ ὁ κύριος ἡμῶν Ἰησοῦς Χριστὸς καὶ ὁ θεὸς ὁ πατὴρ ἡμῶν *ὁ ἀγαπήσας ἡμᾶς καὶ δοὺς παράκλησιν αἰωνίαν καὶ ἐλπίδα ἀγαθὴν ἐν χάριτί* [17]*παρακαλέσαι ὑμῶν τὰς καρδίας καὶ στηρίξαι ἐν παντὶ ἔργῳ καὶ λόγῳ ἀγαθῷ*

[1]Now concerning the coming of our Lord Jesus Christ and our assembling to meet him, we beg you, brethren, [2]not to be quickly shaken in mind or excited, either by spirit or by word, or by letter purporting to be from us, to the effect that the day of the Lord has come. [3]Let no one deceive you in any way; for that day will not come, unless the rebellion comes first, and the man of lawlessness is revealed, the son of perdition, [4]who opposes and exalts himself against every so-called god or object of worship, so that he takes his seat in the temple of God, proclaiming himself to be God. [5]Do you not remember that when I was still with you I told you this? [6]And you know what is restraining him now so that he may be revealed in his time. [7]For the mystery of lawlessness is already at work; only he who now restrains it will do so until he is out of the way. [8]And then the lawless one will be revealed, and the Lord Jesus will slay him with the breath of his mouth and destroy him by his appearing and his coming. [9]The coming of the lawless one by the activity of Satan will be with all power and with pretended signs and wonders, [10]and with all wicked deception for those who are to perish, because they refused to love the truth and so be saved. [11]Therefore God sends upon them a strong delusion, to make them believe what is false, [12]so that all may be condemned who did not believe the truth but had pleasure in unrighteousness. [13]But we are bound to give thanks to God always for you, brethren beloved by the Lord, because God chose you from the beginning to be saved, through sanctification by the Spirit and belief in the truth. [14]To this he called you through our gospel, so that you may obtain the glory of our Lord Jesus Christ. [15]So then, brethren, stand firm and hold to the traditions which you were taught by us, either by word of mouth or by letter. [16]Now may our Lord Jesus Christ himself, and God our Father, who loved us and gave us eternal comfort and good hope through grace, [17]comfort your hearts and establish them in every good work and word.

This "delay" in the Lord's coming is so much part and parcel of God's "plan" (*oikonomia*) that Paul starts his comments regarding "the Lord's day" by strongly prohibiting any teaching in any way, shape, or form that would contradict his unequivocal statement that "that day has not yet come." The strictness of such prohibition even applies to anything purporting to be from Paul himself. For the attentive hearer this is not something novel since early on in Galatians Paul wrote: "But *even if we*, or an angel from heaven, should preach to you a gospel contrary to that which we preached to you, let him be accursed." (1:8) The reason is simple: *in scripture*, the only one whose judgment matters is God himself: "For my thoughts are not your thoughts, neither are your ways my ways, says the Lord. For as the heavens are higher than the earth, so are my ways higher than your ways and my thoughts than your thoughts." (Is 55:8-9) The radicalism of the matter is so extreme that even *the* Apostle now and then phrased his incontrovertibly authoritative teaching in a tentative manner. The most compelling instance of this is his dealing with a new ground that is not covered in scripture, God's writ:

> Now concerning the unmarried, I have no command of the Lord, but I give my opinion as one who by the Lord's mercy is trustworthy … I say this for your own benefit, not to lay any restraint upon you, but to promote good order and to secure your undivided devotion to the Lord ... But in my judgment she is happier if she remains as she is. *And I think that I have the Spirit of God.* (1 Cor 7:25, 35, 40)

Unfortunately, we Christians, baptized into Greek philosophy at the hands of the Alexandrian fathers, got used to speaking of truth and falseness in the absolute as though they were "essential" realities. Even the hands of the translators of the Hebrew original were tied by the "worldview" of the Greek language of the LXX. That is why the Prologue to the Wisdom of Sirach forewarned his readers: "You are urged therefore to read with good will and attention, and to be indulgent in cases where, despite our diligent labor in translating, we may seem to have rendered some phrases imperfectly. For what was originally expressed in Hebrew does not have exactly the same sense when translated into another language. Not only this work, but even the law itself, the prophecies, and the rest of the books differ not a little as originally expressed." The most telling example pertinent to this matter in 2 Thessalonians 2 is how the LXX has two renderings of the same original Hebrew "prophets" (*nebi'im*) in order to differentiate between true prophet and false prophet. Notice how the prepositional *psevdo*— (false) is an addition that is not needed in the original where the meaning, as in all Semitic languages, is dictated by the functionality of the noun or verb that is used within the sentence and context. For the sake of illustration, compare the Hebrew and the Greek in the following passage in Jeremiah where the Hebrew *nebi'im* (prophets) is consistently rendered in the LXX as *psevdoprophētai* (pseudoprophets) instead of simply *prophētai* (prophets):

> The priests and the prophets (*nebi'im; psevdoprophētai*) and all the people heard Jeremiah speaking these words in the house of the Lord. And when Jeremiah had finished speaking all that the Lord had commanded him to speak to all the people, then the priests and the prophets (*nebi'im; psevdoprophētai*) and all the people laid hold of him, saying, "You shall die! Why have you prophesied in the name of the Lord, saying, 'This house shall be like Shiloh, and this city shall be desolate, without inhabitant'?" And all the people gathered about Jeremiah in the house of the Lord. When the princes of Judah heard these things, they came up from the king's house to the house of the Lord and took their seat in the entry of the New Gate of the house of the Lord. Then the priests and the prophets (*nebi'im; psevdoprophētai*) said to the princes and to all the people, "This man deserves the sentence of death, because he has prophesied against this city, as you have heard with your own ears." Then Jeremiah spoke to all the princes and all the people, saying, "The Lord sent me to prophesy against this house and this city all the words you have heard. Now therefore amend your ways and your doings, and obey the voice of the Lord your God, and the Lord will repent of the evil which he has pronounced against you. But as for me, behold, I am in your hands. Do with me as seems good and right to you. Only know for certain that if you put me to death, you will bring innocent blood upon yourselves and upon this city and its inhabitants, for in truth the Lord sent me to you to speak all these

words in your ears." Then the princes and all the people said to the priests and the prophets (*nebi'im; psevdoprophētai*), "This man does not deserve the sentence of death, for he has spoken to us in the name of the Lord our God." (Jer 26:7-16 RSV) (Heb 26:7-16; LXX 33:7-16)[1]

The reason is evident: a false prophet does not reveal his "false" identity, just as an impersonator of a law enforcement agent, whether in real life or movies, does not proclaim his subterfuge. Paul himself had a firsthand experience of the matter in relation to colleagues he dubs as "false apostles" (*psevdapostoloi*), which explains the painful difficult situation in which he was put in Corinth:

> For if some one comes and preaches another Jesus than the one we preached, or if you receive a different spirit from the one you received, or if you accept a different gospel from the one you accepted, you submit to it readily enough ... And what I do I will continue to do, in order to undermine the claim of those who would like to claim that in their boasted mission they work on the same terms as we do. For such men are false apostles, deceitful workmen, disguising themselves as apostles of Christ. And no wonder, for even Satan disguises himself as an angel of light. So it is not strange if his servants also disguise themselves as servants of righteousness. Their end will correspond to their deeds. (2 Cor 11:4, 12-15)

Consequently, one should not be amazed that Paul uses the same terminology of "mystery," "exaltation," "power," "signs," and even "revealing" and "coming" (*parousia*) to speak of "the lawless one" and "son of perdition," as he does to speak of Christ himself (2 Thess 2:3-10). His main point is that one is false while the other is truthful, and God will show the real face of each in *his* time. Yet, for the believers, the urgency lies is that they cannot afford to wait since their judgment will be based on the stand they will have taken. Their only sure way is to abide by the dictates of the Pauline gospel, laid down for them *in this letter* (3:14), knowing

---

[1] See also Jer 6:13; 34:9 (LXX 27:9); 35:1 (LXX 28:1); 36:1, 8 (LXX 29:1, 8); and Zech 1:2.

full well that that gospel will function as the muster against which everyone shall be judged (Rom 2:16): "To this he called you through our gospel, so that you may obtain the glory of our Lord Jesus Christ. So then, brethren, stand firm and hold to the traditions which you were taught by us, either by word of mouth or by letter." (2 Thess 2:14-15)

The reference to "the traditions" heard by the Thessalonians is a literary device meant to keep them pinned to the contents of the letter being written. It is not a free rein to instate a "living oral tradition" made up by men to promote their own thought and ways, as is evident in the many "Christian" traditions.[2] It is no wonder then that Paul ends his central chapter on the following tone: "Now may our Lord Jesus Christ himself, and God our Father, who loved us and gave us eternal comfort and good hope through grace, comfort your hearts and establish them in every good work and word." Notice, first of all, how everything hinges on the "good" hope and, secondly, precedence is given to the *good* work (behavior) that becomes the basis for the *good* word of teaching.

---

[2] An example of this is Christian tradition that titles itself by a term—Orthodoxy—related to "opinion" (from the verb *dokei* [one thinks, opines; it seems to one]); whereas, Paul's gospel is rooted in the *orthopodoun*—the *correct treading with the feet*—according to the Law of the Spirit (See Gal 5:16 and Rom 8:2-8 where the verb *peripatein* [walk] is used). It is therefore unfortunate for us—or rather, scripturally speaking, fortunate—that all the instances of *dokei* in Paul have the negative connotation of thinking wrongly (1 Cor 3:18; 8:2; 11:16; 14:37; Gal 6:3; Phil 3:4; Heb 12:11), except when it applies to himself as having the Spirit of God (1 Cor 7:40).

Chapter 3

Vv. 1-18 *¹Τὸ λοιπὸν προσεύχεσθέ ἀδελφοί περὶ ἡμῶν ἵνα ὁ λόγος τοῦ κυρίου τρέχῃ καὶ δοξάζηται καθὼς καὶ πρὸς ὑμᾶς ²καὶ ἵνα ῥυσθῶμεν ἀπὸ τῶν ἀτόπων καὶ πονηρῶν ἀνθρώπων· οὐ γὰρ πάντων ἡ πίστις· ³Πιστὸς δέ ἐστιν ὁ κύριος ὃς στηρίξει ὑμᾶς καὶ φυλάξει ἀπὸ τοῦ πονηροῦ ⁴πεποίθαμεν δὲ ἐν κυρίῳ ἐφ᾽ ὑμᾶς ὅτι ἃ παραγγέλλομεν ⸂καὶ⸃ ποιεῖτε καὶ ποιήσετέ ⁵Ὁ δὲ κύριος κατευθύναι ὑμῶν τὰς καρδίας εἰς τὴν ἀγάπην τοῦ θεοῦ καὶ εἰς τὴν ὑπομονὴν τοῦ Χριστοῦ ⁶Παραγγέλλομεν δὲ ὑμῖν ἀδελφοί ἐν ὀνόματι τοῦ κυρίου ⸂ἡμῶν⸃ Ἰησοῦ Χριστοῦ στέλλεσθαι ὑμᾶς ἀπὸ παντὸς ἀδελφοῦ ἀτάκτως περιπατοῦντος καὶ μὴ κατὰ τὴν παράδοσιν ἣν παρελάβοσαν παρ᾽ ἡμῶν ⁷Αὐτοὶ γὰρ οἴδατε πῶς δεῖ μιμεῖσθαι ἡμᾶς ὅτι οὐκ ἠτακτήσαμεν ἐν ὑμῖν ⁸οὐδὲ δωρεὰν ἄρτον ἐφάγομεν παρά τινος ἀλλ᾽ ἐν κόπῳ καὶ μόχθῳ νυκτὸς καὶ ἡμέρας ἐργαζόμενοι πρὸς τὸ μὴ ἐπιβαρῆσαί τινα ὑμῶν· ⁹οὐχ ὅτι οὐκ ἔχομεν ἐξουσίαν ἀλλ᾽ ἵνα ἑαυτοὺς τύπον δῶμεν ὑμῖν εἰς τὸ μιμεῖσθαι ἡμᾶς ¹⁰καὶ γὰρ ὅτε ἦμεν πρὸς ὑμᾶς τοῦτο παρηγγέλλομεν ὑμῖν ὅτι εἴ τις οὐ θέλει ἐργάζεσθαι μηδὲ ἐσθιέτω· ¹¹Ἀκούομεν γάρ τινας περιπατοῦντας ἐν ὑμῖν ἀτάκτως μηδὲν ἐργαζομένους ἀλλὰ περιεργαζομένους. ¹²τοῖς δὲ τοιούτοις παραγγέλλομεν καὶ παρακαλοῦμεν ἐν κυρίῳ Ἰησοῦ Χριστῷ ἵνα μετὰ ἡσυχίας ἐργαζόμενοι τὸν ἑαυτῶν ἄρτον ἐσθίωσιν· ¹³ὑμεῖς δέ ἀδελφοί μὴ ἐγκακήσητε καλοποιοῦντες· ¹⁴Εἰ δέ τις οὐχ ὑπακούει τῷ λόγῳ ἡμῶν διὰ τῆς ἐπιστολῆς τοῦτον σημειοῦσθε μὴ συναναμίγνυσθαι αὐτῷ ἵνα ἐντραπῇ· ¹⁵καὶ μὴ ὡς ἐχθρὸν ἡγεῖσθέ ἀλλὰ νουθετεῖτε ὡς ἀδελφόν· ¹⁶Αὐτὸς δὲ ὁ κύριος τῆς εἰρήνης δῴη ὑμῖν τὴν εἰρήνην διὰ παντὸς ἐν παντὶ τρόπῳ· ὁ κύριος μετὰ πάντων ὑμῶν· ¹⁷Ὁ ἀσπασμὸς τῇ ἐμῇ χειρὶ Παύλου ὅ ἐστιν σημεῖον ἐν πάσῃ ἐπιστολῇ· οὕτως γράφω· ¹⁸Ἡ χάρις τοῦ κυρίου ἡμῶν Ἰησοῦ Χριστοῦ μετὰ πάντων ὑμῶν·*

[1]Finally, brethren, pray for us, that the word of the Lord may speed on and triumph, as it did among you, [2]and that we may be delivered from wicked and evil men; for not all have faith. [3]But the Lord is faithful; he will strengthen you and guard you from evil. [4]And we have confidence in the Lord about you, that you are doing and will do the things which we command. [5]May the Lord direct your hearts to the love of God and to the steadfastness of Christ. [6]Now we command you, brethren, in the name of our Lord Jesus Christ, that you keep away from any brother who is living in idleness and not in accord with the tradition that you received from us. [7]For you yourselves know how you ought to imitate us; we were not idle when we were with you, [8]we did not eat any one's bread without paying, but with toil and labor we worked night and day, that we might not burden any of you. [9]It was not because we have not that right, but to give you in our conduct an example to imitate. [10]For even when we were with you, we gave you this command: If any one will not work, let him not eat. [11]For we hear that some of you are living in idleness, mere busybodies, not doing any work. [12]Now such persons we command and exhort in the Lord Jesus Christ to do their work in quietness and to earn their own living. [13]Brethren, do not be weary in well-doing. [14]If any one refuses to obey what we say in this letter, note that man, and have nothing to do with him, that he may be ashamed. [15]Do not look on him as an enemy, but warn him as a brother. [16]Now may the Lord of peace himself give you peace at all times in all ways. The Lord be with you all. [17]I, Paul, write this greeting with my own hand. This is the mark in every letter of mine; it is the way I write. [18]The grace of our Lord Jesus Christ be with you all.

It is only befitting that the last correspondence of the Pauline corpus to churches sounds as an echo of the Apostle's teaching in his previous letters. Consider the following features:

- Paul's first request is that prayer be made so "that the word of the Lord may speed (keep running)[1]

---

[1] This is the verb *trekhein* that Paul uses to speak of his apostolic activity which he viewed, among other metaphors, as running a race (1 Cor 9:24, 26; Gal 2:2; Phil 2:16).

on and triumph (*doxazētai*; be glorified)."[2] The same idea of "progression" of the gospel is found at its clearest in Philippians: "I want you to know, brethren, that what has happened to me has really served to advance (*prokopē*) the gospel." (1:12).

- The confidence is in God's faithfulness to his plan: "But the Lord is faithful (*pistos*); he will strengthen you and guard you from evil. And we have confidence (*pepeithamen*)[3] in the Lord about you, that you are doing and will do the things which we command." (2 Thess 3:3-4). The same thought is found in Philippians: "And I am sure that he who began a good work in you will bring it to completion at the day of Jesus Christ." (1:6)

- Paul refers to the things the Thessalonians are doing and should continue to do as being according to his command (v.4). One cannot help but remember the summons in Galatians to walk according to the dictates of the Spirit (5:16-26), "the law of the Spirit" that alone is the "way" to "life": "For the law of the Spirit of life in Christ Jesus has set me free from the law of sin and death." (Rom 8:2)

- The verb "command" (*parangellomen*) is repeated three more times (2 Thess 3:6, 10, 12) bringing its instances in a short passage (vv.4-12) to four. The

---

[2] As in 1:12: "so that the name of our Lord Jesus may be glorified (*endoxasthē*) in you, and you in him."

[3] The verbs *pistevō* and *peithomai* bear the same connotation. See Galatians 5:6-8: "For in Christ Jesus neither circumcision nor uncircumcision is of any avail, but faith (*pistis*) working through love. You were running (*Etrekhete*) well; who hindered you from obeying (*peithesthai*; trusting) the truth? This persuasion (*peismonē*, from the same root as *peithesthai*) is not from him who calls you."

hearers cannot miss that it is the universality of the teaching that is underscored. This is appropriate in a letter that recapitulates the entire Pauline teaching by presenting it in three similar chapters.[4] This being the case, it is only fitting that the last instance of *parangellomen* is immediately followed with "If any one refuses to obey what we say (*to logo hēmōn*; our word [which is the Pauline gospel]) *in this letter*," which in turn prepares for the concluding "in every letter of mine" (v.17).

- The centrality of doing comes back in no uncertain terms where "not being weary in well-doing (*kalopoiountes*; doing the good)" is referring to "working" and "not being idle": "For even when we were with you, we gave you this command: If any one will not work (*ergazesthai*), let him not eat. For we hear that some of you are living *in idleness* (*ataktōs*; in an disorderly manner), mere busybodies, not doing any *work* (*ergazomenous*). Now such persons we command and exhort in the Lord Jesus Christ to do their *work* (*ergazomenoi*) in quietness and *to earn their own living* (*ton eavtōn arton esthiōsin*; eating their own bread). Brethren, do not be weary in well-doing (*mē enkakēsēte kaliopoiountes*)." (vv.10-13) When this passage is heard in conjunction with the previous letter to the same Thessalonians, the hearer cannot but conclude that "working" is "working with one's hands" (*ergazesthai tais [idiais] khersin hymōn*), especially when followed immediately with "as we charged you" (*kathōs hymin parēngeilamen*)[5] (1 Thess 4:11) The same passage (2 Thess 3:10-13)

---

[4] See above my comments on the numeral three that is indicative of the divine fullness as well as indeedness.

[5] The aorist tense of *parangellomen*.

recalls 1 Corinthians and Galatians. The adverb *ataktōs* (disorderly) is the opposite of the phrase *kata taxin* (according to order; orderly) that is heard in 1 Corinthians 14: "but all things should be done decently and in order (*kata taxin*)." (v.40)[6] As for the phrase *mē enkakēsēte kaliopoiountes*, it brings to mind to *de kalon poiountes mē enkakōmen* ("And let us not grow weary in well-doing;" Gal 6:9).

- That 1 Corinthians and Galatians are on the author's mind here is sealed in the sequence of 2 Thessalonians 3:14-15. The harsh directive, "If any one refuses to obey what we say in this letter, note that man, and have nothing to do with him, that he may be ashamed" (v.14), recalls 1 Corinthians 5:1-7. "Do not look on him as an enemy, but warn him as a brother" (2 Thess 3:15) brings to mind Galatians 6:1: "Brethren, if a man is overtaken in any trespass, you who are spiritual should restore him in a spirit of gentleness."

- Given that the last two chapters of Galatians are heavily on the mind of the author of 2 Thessalonians, the hearers cannot escape the distinct impression that the additional "This is the mark in every letter of mine" after "I, Paul, write this greeting with my own hand; it is the way I write" (3:17) is meant as the "seal" that Paul's teaching is now "scripturalized" as a writ[7] for all coming ages, and that they are invited to recall the

---

[6] See also "For though I am absent in body, yet I am with you in spirit, rejoicing to see your *good order* (*taxin*) and the firmness of your faith in Christ" (Col 2:5).

[7] My readers are reminded that the Greek verb *graphō* (write) and noun *graphē* (scripture) are from the same root *graph*—. The same applies to the Latin verb *scribo* (write) and noun *scriptura*.

ending of Galatians, "Henceforth let no man trouble me; for I bear on my body the marks of Jesus" (6:17) that is squeezed between the mention of peace (Gal 6:16) and that of grace (Gal 6:18), just as it is here (2 Thess 3:16 [peace] and 18 [grace]).

Excursus 1

The Gospel's Function

In the Introduction I surmised that the gospel preached by Paul not only forewarns of the Lord's coming, but also "produces" or at least "triggers" it. The basis for this surmise is found in the following passage:

> ¹Now concerning the coming of our Lord Jesus Christ and our assembling to meet him, we beg you, brethren, ²not to be quickly shaken in mind or excited, either by spirit or by word, or by letter purporting to be from us, to the effect that the day of the Lord has come. ³Let no one deceive you in any way; for that day will not come, unless the rebellion comes first, and the man of lawlessness (*anomias*) is revealed, the son of perdition, ⁴who opposes and exalts himself against every so-called god or object of worship, so that he takes his seat in the temple of God, proclaiming himself to be God. ⁵Do you not remember that when I was still with you I told you this? ⁶And you know what is restraining (*to katekhon*) him now so that he may be revealed in his time. ⁷For the mystery of lawlessness (*anomias*) is already at work; only he who now restrains (*ho katekhōn*) it will do so until he is out of the way. ⁸And then the lawless one (*anomos*) will be revealed, and the Lord Jesus will slay him with the breath of his mouth and destroy him by his appearing and his coming. (2 Thess 2:1-8)

The coming of the Lord will not take place until the "anti-god," the "lawless one," is revealed in power so that the Lord would show everyone that he, the Lord, can overpower that false god who has been trying to lure those who had put their trust in the gospel's teaching:

> ⁹The coming of the lawless one by the activity of Satan will be with all power and with pretended signs and wonders, ¹⁰and with all wicked (*adikias*) deception for those who are to perish, because they refused to love the truth and so be saved. ¹¹Therefore God sends upon them a strong delusion, to make them believe what is false, ¹²so that all may be condemned who did not believe the truth but

had pleasure in unrighteousness (*adikia*). [13]But we are bound to give thanks to God always for you, brethren beloved by the Lord, because God chose you from the beginning to be saved, through sanctification by the Spirit and belief in the truth. *[14]To this he called you through our gospel, so that you may obtain the glory of our Lord Jesus Christ.* [15]So then, brethren, stand firm and hold to the traditions which you were taught by us, either by word of mouth or by letter. (vv.9-15)

Given that *anomia* (lawlessness) and *adikia* (unrighteousness) go hand in hand, and that the law determines what is (up)right,[1] it ensues that the real and ultimate battle is between God (vv.10, 11, 13) and Satan (v.9) whose mediums are the Lord Jesus Christ (v.13) and the "lawless one" (*anomos*; v.8), respectively. Ultimately, it is God who grants power to the Lord to overcome the "man of lawlessness," and by the same token grants deliverance to those who will have put their trust in *God's* call through *Paul's* gospel (v.14). This gospel, in turn and by the same token, is the medium of God's judgement (v.11-12), as Paul underscored in Romans:

> For God shows no partiality. All who have sinned without the law will also perish without the law, and all who have sinned under the law will be judged by the law. For it is not the hearers of the law who are righteous before God, but the doers of the law who will be justified. When Gentiles who have not the law do by nature what the law requires, they are a law to themselves, even though they do not have the law. They show that what the law requires is written on their hearts, while their conscience also bears witness and their conflicting thoughts accuse or perhaps excuse them *on that day when, according to my gospel, God judges the secrets of men by Christ Jesus.* (Rom 2:11-16)

Through teaching the gospel to the Romans (1:1-15), Paul is trying to ensure both their righteousness and salvation on judgement day (vv.16-17; see also 2 Thess 2:10-12). However, in this same letter, Paul is delaying the coming of that day through his plan to cover

---

[1] See Rom 1-3.

the westernmost parts of the Roman empire (Rom 15:18-24) so that not only the citizens of Rome but also all the Gentiles, whom the Romans are only a part of, become "obedient" (v.18): "through whom we have received grace and apostleship to bring about the obedience of faith for the sake of his name among all the nations, *including yourselves* (*en hois kai hymeis*; among whom also yourselves) who are called to belong to Jesus Christ" (Rom 1:5-6). This is only fair since God is a "righteous"—and not whimsical— judge: "But if our wickedness serves to show the justice of God, what shall we say? That God is unjust to inflict wrath on us? (I speak in a human way.) By no means! For then how could God judge the world?" (Rom 3:5-6) And unless God gives a fair chance to the Gentiles to be privy to his "oracles" (*logia*) with which he "entrusted the Jews" (v.2) through Paul's conveying those "oracles" (*logia*) through the gospel "word" (*logos*) to those Gentiles, God would be unfair and, ultimately, unjust.[2] The obvious reason is stated by Paul himself at the close of the same chapter: "Or is God the God of Jews only? Is he not the God of Gentiles also? Yes, of Gentiles also, since God is one; and he will justify the circumcised on the ground of their faith and the uncircumcised through their faith." (Rom 3:29-30)

It is this scenario that is played again in 2 Thessalonians 2. It is the gospel preaching, which is proclaiming the "coming" of the Lord, that is also restraining the "revealing" of the "lawless one" which is the prelude to the "revealing" of the Lord. It is interesting, in this regard, that the author is obliquely hinting at this reality in his use of the grammatically neuter "what is restraining" (*to katekhon*) and the grammatically masculine "he who now restrains" (*ho katekhōn*) in immediate sequence (vv.6 and 7). The unbiased hearer who has already been subjected to the entire gamut of the Pauline letters to churches would readily conclude that the only way to make "functional" sense of this

---

[2] Hence the compelling story of the Book of Jonah as a lesson in equanimity—if not outright mercy—to the recalcitrant Jonah!

strangeness is to "hear" the "neuter" *to katekhon* as referring to the equally neuter *to evangelion* (the gospel) or *to kērygma* (the heralding, preaching),[3] and the "masculine" *ho katekhōn* to its equally masculine counterpart *ho logos* (the [gospel] word) or either the masculine *ho apostolos* (the apostle) or *ho kēryssōn* (the herald).[4]

[3] Rom 16:25; 1 Cor 1:21; 2:4; 15:14; 2 Tim 4:17; Titus 1:3.
[4] Rom 10:14-15.

Excursus 2

Silvanus

Among the major names in the New Testament, Silvanus is in the same category as Paul, Mark, and Luke in that they are all of Latin, rather than Greek or Hebrew, provenance. The use of the Latin names Paul, Mark, and Luke indicates that, when writing, the New Testament authors had the Roman empire and all its inhabitants in their purview. In this regard Silvanus can hardly compare with them since he is no author, except in an oblique manner, just as Timothy and Sosthenes are:

> Paul, called by the will of God to be an apostle of Christ Jesus, and our brother Sosthenes (1 Cor 1:1)

> Paul, an apostle of Christ Jesus by the will of God, and Timothy our brother (2 Cor 1:1)

> Paul and Timothy, servants of Christ Jesus (Phil 1:1)

> Paul, an apostle of Christ Jesus by the will of God, and Timothy our brother (Col 1:1)

> Paul, a prisoner for Christ Jesus, and Timothy our brother (Philem 1:1)

Still Timothy and Sosthenes are Greek names, whereas Silvanus is clearly Latin. Its meaning is "related to forest (Latin *silva*)," and is the name of the god Silvanus, the Roman deity of forest and fields. In my commentary on 1 Corinthians I discussed the function of Sosthenes within the parameters of that letter. He is identified as a "brother" (1:1). The Greek *Sōsthenēs* is a composite of *sōs* (healthy, from the verb *sōzō* whose meaning is "maintain in safety" and thus "save") and *sthenēs* (from *sthenos* whose meaning is "physical strength" and whose opposite is *astheneia* denoting "lack of strength," "weakness," "sickness"). Someone who is lacking *sthenos* is an *asthenēs* (weak, sick). The noun *astheneia*, and

141

more so the adjective *asthenēs*, are used profusely in 1 Corinthians, especially in the debate concerning the attitudes of the "strong" and the "weak" about what food to eat or what to abstain from at table fellowship (8:7-13).[1] The weak brother is clearly the Jew who is bound by dietary rules.[2] Thus it would appear that Sosthenes stands for a Jew who was saved (healed, made whole), and became a "brother" worthy, in spite of his weakness (*astheneia*), to be cited next to Paul himself as putative co-author of the letter. Paul will use the meaning of the name Sosthenes throughout the letter in order to tame the arrogance of the Gentile Corinthians, just as he endeavored to do with the Gentile Romans in Romans (9-11 and 12-15). My understanding that Sosthenes is a Jew finds direct support in scripture since the only other occurrence of that name is found in Acts where we hear it in conjunction with Paul's activity in Corinth: "And they all seized Sosthenes, the ruler of the synagogue, and beat him in front of the tribunal." (Acts 18:17)

However, compared to Sosthenes who is merely a literary device, so to speak, Silvanus is referred to in a way that reflects both his apostolic activity as a co-adjutant of Paul on par with Timothy and, more importantly, his being a scriptural "writer":

> For the Son of God, Jesus Christ, whom we preached among you, Silvanus and Timothy and I, was not Yes and No; but in him it is always Yes. (2 Cor 1:20)

> By Silvanus, a faithful brother as I regard him, I have written briefly to you, exhorting and declaring that this is the true grace of God; stand fast in it. She who is at Babylon, who is likewise chosen, sends you greetings; and so does my son Mark. (1 Pet 5:12-13)

In 1 Peter, Silvanus is enhanced in that he is chosen to be the amanuensis over Peter's son "Mark," the Gospel "writer." So, to find Silvanus sharing the place of honor as "co-author" in the

---

[1] Paul's instructions in this regard took a good share of his letter to the Romans as well (14:1-15).

[2] See my comments on Rom 14:1-15 in *C-Rom* 250-8.

Thessalonian correspondence, together with Timothy, Paul's traditional "co-author" (2 Cor, Phil, Col, Philem), is no trifling matter, especially when one considers that his name is introduced *before* that of Timothy (1 Thess 1:1; 2 Thess 1:1).

In Acts the name of the one who was active in Corinth with Timothy (2 Cor 1:19) is presented under the Grecized version Silas (*Silas*; Acts 18:5)[3] rather than the Latin *Silvanus* whose Greek transliteration is *Silouanos*.[4] This parallels the rendering of the Latin *Lucius* or *Lucianus* (related to *lux* [light]) into its Grecized shorter form *Loukas* (Luke) instead of *Loukianos*. This, in turn, brings to the fore two matters to be dealt with. On the one hand, Silas appears in Acts 15 (vv.22, 27, 32, 40) as one of the special emissaries of the Jerusalemite leadership under James, long before Timothy's introduction in 16:1-3, and subsequently functions as Paul's sole adjutant in Philippi (vv.19, 25, 29) and Thessalonica (17:4, 10, 14), both in Macedonia. During this period, Timothy is not mentioned at all until the concluding verse of the Thessalonian episode where he is brought in as second in line to Silas: "Then the brethren immediately sent Paul off on his way to the sea, but Silas and Timothy remained there. Those who conducted Paul brought him as far as Athens; and receiving a command for Silas and Timothy to come to him as soon as possible, they departed." (vv.14-15) It is only in conjunction with Paul's activity in Corinth (18:1-21) that both Silas and Timothy— in this order—are mentioned as co-adjutants of Paul right from the beginning: "When Silas and Timothy arrived from Macedonia, Paul was occupied with preaching, testifying to the Jews that the Christ was Jesus." (v.5).

Before trying to solve the puzzle of Silvanus-Silas, an aside is in order here about another puzzle concerning another enigmatic

---

[3] The correspondence between the instance in 2 Corinthians and the Book of Acts is evident in the sequence of the pair of names: "Silvanus and Timothy" (2 Cor 1:19) and "Silas and Timothy" (Acts 17:14, 15; 18:5).

[4] 2 Cor 1:19; 1 Thess 1:1; 2 Thess 1:1; 1 Pet 5:12.

person, Apollos, who was active in Corinth at the same time as Silas was (Acts 18:24; 19:1) and, more importantly, whose work there was given a place of honor, on par with Paul, in the first letter addressed to the church residing in that city (1:12; 3:4, 5, 6, 22; 4:6; 16:12). Is it a mere coincidence that both Silas and Apollos, both prominent and both Jews,[5] were active concomitantly in Corinth as top co-adjutants of Paul? I think not. I am convinced that both of them are functionally different stand-ins for Silvanus, Paul's co-sender of 1 and 2 Thessalonians and the writer of 1 Peter.

The most expedient approach to build up this argument is to point out that both Silas and Apollos disappear from the purview of Acts at the end of Paul's lengthy Corinthian stay of eighteen months (18:11). The last mention of Silas is in 18:5 and that of Apollos in 19:1. It is only Timothy, recruited at the beginning of chapter 16 (vv.1-3), who remains in Paul's company during his subsequent apostolic journeys through Macedonia and Greece-Achaia (20:1-4).[6] It is as though Silas and Apollos suddenly became *personae non gratae*. Considering Paul's intransigence when it came to the "truth of the (one) gospel" (Gal 1:6-9; 2:5, 14), one can safely surmise that the case of those adjutants must have been similar to that of Mark who was discharged of his duties for having shown signs of vacillation in his commitment to the cause of the Pauline gospel:

> And after some days Paul said to Barnabas, "Come, let us return and visit the brethren in every city where we proclaimed the word of the Lord, and see how they are." And Barnabas wanted to take with them John called Mark. But Paul thought best not to take with them one who had withdrawn from them in Pamphylia, and had not gone with them to the work. And there arose a sharp contention, so that they separated from each other; Barnabas took

---

[5] Acts 16:19-20 (also 15:22, 27, 32) for Silas and 18:24 for Apollos.

[6] If one adds that the enigmatic "Three Taverns" at the gates of Rome (Acts 28:15) is an oblique reference to the three T's, Timothy, Tychicus, and Trophimus (20:4), then Timothy will have accompanied Paul all the way to Rome.

Mark with him and sailed away to Cyprus, but Paul chose Silas and departed, being commended by the brethren to the grace of the Lord. And he went through Syria and Cilicia, strengthening the churches. (Acts 15:36-41)

Given the mention of Silas in this context, the hearers of Acts are prepared to sense that the same fate would befall Silas should he start acting as Mark did, and from there a second step would be to surmise that his sudden disappearance from the story's horizon had to do with his "betrayal" of the gospel at some point during his activity in Corinth. *Mutatis mutandis* one can draw the same conclusion regarding Apollos.

Still, what is the relation between Silas and Apollos? The original hearers, familiar with Greek mythology, would have immediately guessed the latter name was an intentional reference to the Greek god Apollo, especially when one considers that both use the Greek letter ω (omega, transliterated as *ō*) at the end of each names: *Apollōs* (Ἀπολλῶς in Acts and 1 Corinthians) and *Apollōn* (Ἀπολλῶν the god). Apollo's "betrayal" of the apostolic mission to Corinth, the capital of the Roman province Achaia that corresponded to the area of ancient Greece, would then correspond to the god Apollo's stand against the Greeks during the Trojan war on two counts. First of all, he shot arrows infected with the plague into the Greek encampment in retribution for Agamemnon's insult to Chryses, a priest of Apollo. Secondly, Apollo guided the arrow of Paris' bow into Achilles' heel. The Greek verb *syl(a)ō* primarily means "pull an arrow out of the quiver" and, by extension, "disarm, despoil an enemy (by emptying the quiver of its arrows)." So it stands to reason that the New Testament authors played on Sylvanus,[7] the alternate form of the god Silvanus, to link Silas with anti-gospel behavior. Still they coined the name Silas instead of Sylas to preserve, in the hearer's mind, that Silas and Silvanus are opposite sides of the

---

[7] Which is used in the name of the State of Pennsylvania, the *sylvania* (wooded expanse) of Penn.

same coin, thus underscoring the *perversion* of the gospel under the guise of presenting another *version* of it: "I am astonished that you are so quickly deserting him who called you in the grace of Christ and turning to a different gospel—not that there is another gospel, but there are some who trouble you and want to pervert the gospel of Christ." (Gal 1:6-7). This understanding is borne out by an analysis of the three occurrences of the verbal root *syl—* in the New Testament:

> For you have brought these men here who are neither sacrilegious (*hierosylous*; robbers of temples) nor blasphemers of our goddess. (Act 19:37)

> you then who teach others, will you not teach yourself? While you preach against stealing, do you steal? You who say that one must not commit adultery, do you commit adultery? You who abhor idols, do you rob temples (*hierosyleis*)? You who boast in the law, do you dishonor God by breaking the law? For, as it is written, "The name of God is blasphemed among the Gentiles because of you." (Rom 2:21-24)

> Did I commit a sin in abasing myself so that you might be exalted, because I preached God's gospel without cost to you? I robbed (*esylēsa*) other churches by accepting support from them in order to serve (*diakonian*; minister to) you. (2 Cor 11:7-8)

In Romans 2 the person under criticism is the Jew who boasts that he is entrusted with the Law (3:2) and yet behaves similarly to a Gentile. In this context we hear of a Jew who takes the opportunity of the Law's teaching concerning the false deities in order to "rob" their temples for his own benefit (2:22). The outcome is that "as it is written, 'The name of God is blasphemed among the Gentiles because of you.'" The hypocrisy of such behavior lies in that the dictates of the Law are addressed primarily to the insiders: "Now we know that whatever the law says it speaks to those who are under the law" (Rom 3:19)—those to whom it was entrusted—and only secondarily to the outsiders

(Josh 8:32-35).[8] This understanding of the root *ierosyl*— sheds light on its use in Acts where Paul defends himself and his companions as not being "temple robbers" and, no less, in conjunction with such an accusation being leveled against them by the servers of the temple of Artemis, Apollo's twin sister. Paul's preaching the gospel in Ephesus, Artemis' city, did not give free rein to do so. Rather his preaching there was to invite Artemis' followers to "turn to God from idols and in order to serve a living and true God" (1 Thess 1:9), should they decide of their own free will to do so. It thus makes sense that the demise of the Jew Silas was due to his turnabout, at one point, following the example of Peter and Barnabas at Antioch (Gal 2:11-14), under the pressure of "certain men from James" (v.12). What makes this scenario plausible is that Silas is introduced as someone under the aegis of James (Acts 15:13) and the Jerusalemite leadership (v.22) and, more specifically, a close companion of "Judah" (vv.27, 32) whence the name Jew (Judahite) originates. In other words, when the Pauline gospel is contravened, the Jew Silas fares no better than his counterpart Apollos who emulates the god Apollo in his vengeful behavior. As for Paul, he pressures not the outsiders but his own churches by "robbing" them in order to fulfill his apostolic ministry in Corinth.

Just as John (a Semitic Hebrew name), Paul and Barnabas' helper, who, at one point, vacillated regarding the Pauline gospel, was "salvaged" under his Latin name Mark (12:12, 25; 15:37) by both Paul (Col 4:10) and Peter (1 Pet 5:13), so also the Greek named Jew Silas, aka, Apollos, was "salvaged" out of his betrayal of the gospel under his Latin (and thus Gentile) name Silvanus. Such a pattern is classic in the New Testament especially when one considers that Saul (a Semitic Hebrew name) was "salvaged" under the Latin (and thus Gentile) name *Paulus* and Cephas (an Aramaic—Semitic—name) was "salvaged" under the Greek (and

---

[8] A similar behavior is rampant in all Christian traditions whereby, after having "appropriated" scripture as their own, the Christians, originally Gentiles by and large, start applying its "blessings" to themselves and its "curses" to the "outsiders."

thus Gentile) name *Petros*. The choice of Silvanus was dictated because of its reference to the Roman god Silvanus, the deity of forests and fields, which corresponds to the description of Apollos' activity (1 Cor 3:5-9). The choice of the name reflects the taming of Rome through the gospel. As the Roman deity of the forests and fields, it was only fitting that its character in the New Testament narrative be someone who would be the helper of Paul in sowing the "seed" of the gospel and planting it in a field where it would blossom as the "church of God":

> Paul, called by the will of God to be an apostle of Christ Jesus, and our brother Sosthenes, to the church of God which is at Corinth, to those sanctified in Christ Jesus, called to be saints together with all those who in every place call on the name of our Lord Jesus Christ, both their Lord and ours (1 Cor 1:1-2)

> Paul, an apostle of Christ Jesus by the will of God, and Timothy our brother. To the church of God which is at Corinth, with all the saints who are in the whole of Achaia (2 Cor 1:1)

> What then is Apollos? What is Paul? Servants through whom you believed, as the Lord assigned to each. I planted, Apollos watered, but God gave the growth. So neither he who plants nor he who waters is anything, but only God who gives the growth. He who plants and he who waters are equal, and each shall receive his wages according to his labor. For we are God's fellow workers; you are God's field, God's building.[9] (1 Cor 3:5-9)

> Who serves as a soldier at his own expense? Who plants a vineyard without eating any of its fruit? Who tends a flock without getting some of the milk? Do I say this on human authority? Does not the law say the same? For it is written in the law of Moses, "You shall not muzzle an ox when it is treading out the grain." Is it for oxen

---

[9] Notice how Paul gives precedence to "field" over "building." This goes hand in hand with his belittling of Greek (human) wisdom (philosophy) in that letter and his upholding God's wisdom revealed in the apparent "folly" of the gospel preaching (1 Cor 1-2). In turn, the church "building" is not a Greek city stone building (*oikos*) but rather one made of human beings (3:10-17), just as is the case in a Roman *domus* (*oikos*, house[hold]).

that God is concerned? Does he not speak entirely for our sake? It was written for our sake, because the plowman should plow in hope and the thresher thresh in hope of a share in the crop. If we have sown spiritual good among you, is it too much if we reap your material benefits? (1 Cor 9:7-11)

The conclusion is unavoidable: the recalcitrant Apollos was tamed as Silvanus into a ministry (*diakonian*) similar to that of Paul (1 Cor 3) in the service of God's field, and by the same token Silvanus, the Roman deity, was tamed in the service of the gospel in Corinth, the capital of Achaia-Greece, just as the Greek deities, the *Dioscuroi*, the Twin Brothers, were tamed into the service of the same gospel, guiding Paul's ship to the capital of the Roman empire (Acts 28:11). Still the highest place of honor granted Silvanus is his position after Paul and *before* Timothy—who has already appeared in 2 Corinthians, Philippians, and Colossians— in the two letters that close the Pauline corpus of epistles to churches and addressed "to the church of the Thessalonians in God the Father and the Lord Jesus Christ" (1 Thess 1:1; 2 Thess 1:1), that is to say, to the church of the citizens of the capital of Macedonia, the land of Alexander of Macedon whose unparalleled feat around the Syrian Wilderness triggered the production of scripture. This time around the Pauline gospel is handed to them *twice* (in two letters)—at the hand of Paul together with Silvanus (first) and Timothy. Silvanus' place of honor is sealed by the endorsement of Peter, the "other" *apostle* (Gal 2:8), who names Silvanus his amanuensis (1 Pet 5:12).